CORRUPTION

EXPOSED

Corruption Exposed

Examining its Impact on Industries and Communities

Authors
Austin Mardon
Muzammil Bin Younus, Jennifer Nguyen, Ivy Truong,
Maria Ivanova, Aidan Lang, Khushi Shah, Madhumita Nathani,
Bareeha Shamsi, Marcile Wilmot

Edited by
Andrei Kazakoff
Catherine Mardon

Copyright © 2023 by Austin Mardon

All rights reserved. This book or any portion thereof may not be reproduced or used in any manner whatsoever without the express written permission of the publisher except for the use of brief quotations in a book review or scholarly journal.
First Printing: 2023

Cover Design and typeset by Clare Dalton

Print ISBN 978-1-77369-894-6
Ebook ISBN 978-1-77369-895-3

        Golden Meteorite Press
        103 11919 82 St NW
        Edmonton, AB T5B 2W3
        www.goldenmeteoritepress.com

Contents

Introduction	9
Corruption and the Banking Sector	11
Nestlé's Scandalous History of Corruption Towards Health In Developed and Developing Nations	25
Corruption in the Pharmaceutical Company	41
The Impact of Corruption on Canada's Indigenous Community	55
Social Mechanisms Facilitating Police Corruption in Canada	69
Corruption and Education	83
Corruption's Impact on Economic Development	95
The Effects of Corruption on National Security	111
Corruption in the Workplace	123
Conclusion	137

Introduction

Welcome to "Corruption", a book that aims to shed light on the various forms of corruption that plague our society. In these pages, we will explore the various ways in which corruption can manifest itself, from the baking sector to indigenous communities, and from the workplace to national security. We will be delving into the root causes of corruption and explore the various mechanisms that have been employed to address it.

Corruption and the Banking Sector

Muzammil Bin Younus

Introduction

Banks play an important role in the capital allocation process and thus the economic development of a country (Houston et al., 2010). Banking systems that operate efficiently facilitate the channeling and monitoring of savings to the most productive investment projects, which enhances the performance of economies (Barth et al., 2008). Banks matter for countries at all stages of development in all parts of the world (Barth et al., 2008). However, especially for developing and emerging economies, since banks are the major source of external finance for business firms, a well-functioning banking system has the potential to help reduce income inequality and poverty (Barth et al., 2008).

However, unfortunately, the banking systems are susceptible to corruption, which undermines their primary function of allocating scarce capital efficiently (Barth et al., 2008). As bank credit is an important driving force for economic growth, the focus of this chapter is to understand the impact of corruption in the banking system, both direct and indirect.

Corruption exists despite the efforts of national and international controlling bodies such as central banks, Organization for Economic

Cooperation and Development (OECD) conventions, International Monetary Fund (IMF) and other agencies (Bahoo, 2020). According to Global Witness Organization, corrupt members of the society such as businesspeople, government officials, dictators, warlords and other criminals always need a bank to hide and lander their looted money (Bahoo, 2020). Consequently, banks along with other financial institutions play a key role in hiding the illegal money (Bahoo, 2020). Involvement of banks in corrupt activities and incompetent bank officials has resulted in bankruptcy of major financial institutions in the past, such as Bear Stearns, Lehman Brothers and Washington Mutual (Bahoo, 2020). These bank scandals have led to investigations and research into corruption in banks by regulatory bodies mentioned earlier.

Bank scandals have also ignited the interest of and led to investigations by academic researchers (Bahoo, 2020). As per (Bahoo, 2020), who conducted a bibliometric analysis of literature on corruption in banks, there has been a sharp growth trend since 2008 in the number of articles published per year on corruption in banks, which indicates a substantial increase in research in banks due to the bankruptcy scandals of American banking companies in 2008 (Bahoo, 2020). In fact, the number of articles published on the topic of corruption in banks increased from little to none in 1980s to 115 articles in 2018 alone, and 291 articles in the 3-year span between 2017 and 2019 (Bahoo, 2020).

Corruption is a major concern in transition and developing countries because it influences growth and productivity, as well as foreign direct investments (Fungáčová et al., 2015). These countries usually have less developed financial institutions and legal systems, which makes it challenging to sufficiently contain corruption (BECK et al., 2005 and Barth et al., 2008). For example, 461 cases involving bank fraud of more than one million yuans were uncovered in China in 2005 (Barth et al., 2008). In a 2003 Chinese survey of 3561 bank employees, state-owned enterprises, private firms, brokerage houses and rural households,

82% of respondents agreed that corruption was either pervasive or quite pervasive in financial institutions (Chen et al., 2013). Thus 461 cases of bank frauds is assumed to be a small portion of the overall fraud, yet it still amounted to 7.7 billion yuans in fraudulent activity (Barth et al., 2008). Another example is of Turkey, where the banking sector suffered losses close to 6% of the country's GDP in 2000, with political figures running some of the worst performing banks and were involved in corruption (Barth et al., 2008). These examples show how corruption in banks can be quite costly and problematic, particularly for developing and transition countries (Barth et al., 2008). To demonstrate that this issue is not limited to just the countries listed above, result of worldwide enterprise survey by the World Bank shows that corruption of bank officials is considered as an obstacle by 20-40% of the firms in Non-OECD (Organization for Economic Co-operation and Development) countries around the world (Houston et al., 2010).

Corruption can exist in different forms. The following discussion will focus on the different forms of corruption that can exist in the banking industry.

Corruption in the form of bribery in emerging and developing countries

Corruption can exist in the form of bribing bank officials to obtain loans (Fungáčová et al., 2015). Fungáčová et al. (2015) have done an investigation to analyze the effect of bribery on the lending process in transition countries by studying lending activity for a large sample of firms in 14 transition countries. The paper finds that, while bribery contributes to an increase in the amount of lending, it is in the form of short-term bank-debt at the expense of long-term debt (Fungáčová et al., 2015). Long term bank debt is a major source of investment financing that contributes to economic growth, so bribery in bank lending has a negative effect on economic growth (Fungáčová et al., 2015).

Bribery in bank lending can also be connected with higher volume of bad or riskier loans as the bribes may be given to get around risk averse bank officials (Fungáčová et al., 2015). Hence, loans obtained from bribery are more likely to be riskier loans, as shown by several papers which demonstrate a positive relation between corruption and bad loans at the country level (Fungáčová et al., 2015). This results in distortion of allocation of lending resources in favor of corrupt borrowers who do not necessarily have the most profitable investments (Fungáčová et al., 2015). Allocation of funds in such a manner means that fewer funds are available to support more worthy businesses (Barth et al., 2008). Poor and unconnected individuals with innovative ideas are also deprived of funds to improve their economic condition (Barth et al., 2008).

Furthermore, research has shown that corruption of bank officials affects firm growth, however the effect is disproportionate with smaller firms being the most adversely affected (BECK et al., 2005). In fact, research has found that due to corruption and other obstacles, banks are more accessible to large and listed firms than to small and private firms in most countries (Allen et al., 2012). Surveys show that small firms mostly rely on alternative finance such as funds from friends, families, and business partners to fund their investments, operations and growth (Allen et al., 2012). In the survey, about a third of respondents found bank finance costly and difficult to obtain (Allen et al., 2012). Since in developing countries, it is the small and medium firms that contribute the most to the economic growth, obstacles to growth of these small and medium firms are an obstacle to elevation of living standards in the country (Allen et al., 2012).

Corruption in the form of preferential lending

Government ownership of banks is very common in countries other than the United States (DINC, 2005). This makes banks susceptible to political influence and corruption. With government ownership of banks, the government's role in finance is not limited to just the regulation and enforcement functions (DINC, 2005). On one hand, government ownership of banks is considered to be a positive by some as it is commonly claimed that these banks facilitate financing of projects that private banks are unable or unwilling to finance, particularly those that could contribute to economic development (DINC, 2005). However, these banks can be used by politicians to further their own political goals (DINC, 2005). They can also be used by the political elite to maintain and increase its power through the control of financial resources (DINC, 2005). This can be credited to findings of several academic papers which document that government ownership of banks is associated with lower economic growth (DINC, 2005).

Dinc (2005) provides evidence that government-owned banks increase their lending in election years, which indicates that politics influence the actions taken by the government owned banks (DINC, 2005). There is also evidence of politicians using government owned banks to distribute rents to their supporters (DINC, 2005). Claessens et al. (2008) studied 1998 and 2002 Brazilian elections and the impact on bank financing for companies that made campaign contributions (Claessens et al., 2008). It was found that companies that contributed to the elected federal deputies gained preferential access to bank finance and increased their leverage substantially relative to other firms, during the four years following the election (Claessens et al., 2008). Access to preferential finance was even more prevalent for firms that contributed to incumbent candidates and candidates affiliated to the president, suggesting that access to preferential finance also depends on strength of political connection (Claessens et al., 2008). This study also finds that firms have strong incentives to forge alliances with politicians, and that such alliances affect economic outcomes (Claessens et al., 2008). For example, incumbents are likely to use their political influence to oppose financial development because it creates more competition (Claessens et al., 2008). In other words, politicians can use their influence on government-owned banks to reward allies and punish their opponents (DINC, 2005).

Similar patterns were found in other papers for other emerging countries such as in Pakistan and Thailand where politically connected firms borrow twice as much and have 50% higher default rates, with the loans exclusively from government owned banks (Claessens et al., 2008). This is consistent with the belief that loans may be granted for non-financial reasons or as a return of favor, and do not contribute to economic growth (Fungáčová et al., 2015). In fact, some academic papers show that government ownership of banks is associated with a higher likelihood of a banking crisis (DINC, 2005).

Preferential landing by state owned banks is not just limited to developing countries. For example, in Italy, an academic paper found that party affiliation of state-owned bank executives had a positive impact on interest rate discount given by state-owned banks where the associated party is stronger (Cornett et al., 2010).

A theory regarding government-owned banks and the banking crises is provided in (Kane, 2000). The author argues that politicians hope to preserve the rents earned in the past by directing cheap loans to politically powerful parties and sectors (Kane, 2000). In order to do this, they use their influence on state-owned banks to issue preferential (subsidized) loans. This creates un-booked losses for banks, which if grows so big that covering up is no longer possible, results in emergence of a banking crisis due to increasing doubts about government's ability and willingness to guarantee the growing liabilities of the economically insolvent banking system (Cornett et al., 2010). In this event, state-owned banks are usually more impacted due to their larger un-booked losses prior to the crises (Cornett et al., 2010).

As seen in the discussion above, corruption in the form of preferential lending not only results in inefficient allocation of funding or capital, but also impedes the ability of firms, in particular smaller firms, to raise finance through proper banking channels. Preferential lending of State-banks is also associated with higher chances of a more severe banking/financial crisis, which is detrimental to the progress of a developing country. Overall, bank corruption in the form of bribery and preferential lending has a direct impact on credit allocation and cost of borrowing, which will in turn affect the entry and exit for firms and their competitive strategies (Houston et al., 2010). Therefore, both forms of corruptions have a first-order effect on economic development (Houston et al., 2010).

Corruption in the form of regulatory forbearance

Corruption can also exist in the form of regulatory forbearance for banks, such as bank officials bribing politicians to gain such favors (Park, 2012). Government serving as third-party regulator creates opportunities for corruption, as a burdensome regulatory environment increases the opportunities for individuals and firms to bypass regulations through various forms of bribery (Dincer & Gunalp, 2020 and Rose-Ackerman & Palifka, 2016). Regulation can cause corruption directly and indirectly (Dincer & Gunalp, 2020).

Direct mechanism is the power afforded to government officials to extort bribes through their ability to enforce regulations, whether correctly or incorrectly (Dincer & Gunalp, 2020). Dincer & Gunalp (2020) give the example of health inspector, who can use their power to ensure restaurants are abiding to cleanliness or misuse their power to extort bribes in return of allowing restaurants that are not clean to operate, or even from the owners of clean restaurant in order to grant them the certificate. Indirect mechanism is the power afforded to government officials to extort bribes in the form of speed money, through their ability to create red tape (Dincer & Gunalp, 2020). Speed money or "grease payments" is different from bribery as it is paid to speed up the process of something that has be done anyway, instead of bribes which are paid to perform an act someone should not be doing (Deleon, 2015).

As per (Park, 2012), government regulation is regarded as one of the most important tools for corruption in the banking sector. A theory behind this is that greater number of regulations increase opportunities for helping corrupt individuals and firms to evade these regulations (Park, 2012 and Glaeser & Saks, 2006). Since the banking sector is the most regulated sector, according to this theory, it is more vulnerable to public officials using their influence to help connected firms and individuals evade regulations (Park, 2012). Since there are many regulations applicable to the banking sector, and many of these can be manipulated in different ways, this section will only discuss one of the many regulatory requirements to illustrate the some of the effects of corruption in the form of regulatory forbearance.

Some regulatory policies in the banking sector include deposit insurance system and capital regulation (Park, 2012). One of the purposes of these regulations, along with other regulatory measures, is to regulate bank risk management. One of the ways banks mitigate risks to meet these regulatory requirements is through collateral in return of loans, which is a regulatory requirement. However, there is evidence that connected firms can circumvent this requirement which can be seen as direct mechanism of corruption. For example, (Charumilind et al., 2006) find that firms with ties to banks or politicians had better access to bank loans and even financed without collateral in Thailand prior to the IMF crisis (Park, 2012). In addition to needing less collateral, these firms also obtained more long-term loans compared to those without connections (Charumilind et al., 2006).

Result of the research on Thai firms in (Charumilind et al., 2006) suggests a relatively greater importance of collateral on long term financing in nonconnected firms compared to connected firms. For example, looking at the fixed asset ratio, which is the ratio of net fixed assets to total assets, and should normally be associated with long term lending eligibility, it was found that the affect of fixed asset ratio was attenuated or disappeared for firms with strong connections (Charumilind et al., 2006). To exhibit this, (Charumilind et al., 2006) found the affect of fixed asset ratio on long-term borrowing for nonconnected firms to be a dramatic 43.6% and for firms belonging to the richest 60 families to be only 3.86% (Charumilind et al., 2006). Results of the research on Thai firms by (Charumilind et al., 2006) also shows that Thai banks appeared to extend loans based on personal ties and collateral rather than on the basis of expected future cash flow, and in several instances these misallocated loans even bankrupted the banks, as the loans were concentrated amongst only a few influential families who eventually defaulted (Charumilind et al., 2006).

Results of the research in (Charumilind et al., 2006) support the thesis that corruption in the form of regulatory forbearance results in misallocation of funds from normal projects to bad loans, and also typically results in an increase in non-performing loans and deteriorates the quality of bank loans (Park, 2012). As a result, it also results in reduction in the productivity of private investment and leads to lower economic growth (Park, 2012).

Conclusion

Financial institutions such as banks are particularly vulnerable to corruptive practices as they are dealing with cash (Mohamad & Jenkins, 2020). Corruption in the banking industry exists in many different forms, including but not limited to bribery, preferential lending by state-owned banks and evading regulations. Although corruption can exist in many forms, the common ground between all of them are their consequences. Involvement of banks and bank officials in corrupt activities has led to bankruptcy of these banks in the past, both in developed and developing or transition countries. The most notable incident of bank scandals leading to bankruptcy were seen during the Great Recession (between 2007 and 2009), during which many financial institutes were either bailed out or went bankrupt, including some which were too big to fail such as Bear Stearns and Lehman Brothers (Bahoo, 2020).

Although bank corruption existed prior to the Great Recession and have led to bankruptcy of banks and financial crises before, this crisis led to an increase interest on the topic of corruption in the banking system and thus a substantial amount of academic research has been done on the topic since then (Bahoo, 2020). In fact, majority of the research done on bank corruption has been done since 2008 as seen by the number of articles published on the topic in (Bahoo, 2020).

Corruption in Banks affects countries at all stages of development in all parts of the world, however the most affected ones are developing and emerging countries due to lack of adequate laws, objective courts, prudential regulations, and other appropriate institutions to sufficiently contain corruption (Barth et al., 2008). The discussion earlier in this chapter shows that small, private, and politically unconnected firms and entrepreneurs are the biggest victims of corruption in the banking sector as fewer loans are available to support them, due to inefficient allocation of funds which is usually already scarce in developing countries. In fact, banking corruption is so pervasive that the percentage of firms that consider corruption of bank officials to be an obstacle to their business is as high as 19%, 29%, and 45%, respectively, in developing countries in Latin America, Central and Eastern Europe, and East Asia (Chen et al., 2015).

Since small and medium firms contribute most to economic growth in developing countries (Allen et al., 2012), corruption results in reduced growth and improvement in economic conditions of the country. While a well-functioning banking system can help reduce income inequality and poverty (Barth et al., 2008), corruption can have the opposite affect due to preferential access to funding and its negative consequences.

References

Houston, J. F., Lin, C., & Ma, Y. (2010). Media ownership, concentration and corruption in Bank lending. *Journal of Financial Economics*, *100*(2), 326–350. https://doi.org/10.1016/j.jfineco.2010.12.003

Barth, J. R., Lin, C., Lin, P., & Song, F. M. (2008). Corruption in bank lending to firms: Cross-country micro evidence on the beneficial role of competition and Information Sharing. *Journal of Financial Economics*, *91*(3), 361–388. https://doi.org/10.1016/j.jfineco.2008.04.003

Bahoo, S. (2020). Corruption in banks: A bibliometric review and Agenda. *Finance Research Letters*, *35*, 101499. https://doi.org/10.1016/j.frl.2020.101499

Fungáčová, Z., Kochanova, A., & Weill, L. (2015). Does money buy credit? firm-level evidence on bribery and Bank Debt. *World Development*, *68*, 308–322. https://doi.org/10.1016/j.worlddev.2014.12.009

BECK, T. H. O. R. S. T. E. N., DEMIRGÜÇ-KUNT, A. S. L. I., & MAKSIMOVIC, V. O. J. I. S. L. A. V. (2005). Financial and legal constraints to growth: Does firm size matter? *The Journal of Finance*, *60*(1), 137–177. https://doi.org/10.1111/j.1540-6261.2005.00727.x

Allen, F., Chakrabarti, R., De, S., Qian, J. "Q. J., & Qian, M. (2012). Financing firms in India. *Journal of Financial Intermediation, 21*(3), 409–445. https://doi.org/10.1016/j.jfi.2012.01.003

DINC, I. (2005). Politicians and banks: Political influences on government-owned banks in emerging markets. *Journal of Financial Economics, 77*(2), 453–479. https://doi.org/10.1016/j.jfineco.2004.06.011

Claessens, S., Feijen, E., & Laeven, L. (2008). Political connections and preferential access to finance: The Role of Campaign Contributions. *Journal of Financial Economics, 88*(3), 554–580. https://doi.org/10.1016/j.jfineco.2006.11.003

Cornett, M. M., Guo, L., Khaksari, S., & Tehranian, H. (2010). The impact of state ownership on performance differences in privately-owned versus state-owned banks: An international comparison. *Journal of Financial Intermediation, 19*(1), 74–94. https://doi.org/10.1016/j.jfi.2008.09.005

Kane, E. J. (2000). Capital movements, banking insolvency, and silent runs in the Asian Financial Crisis. *Pacific-Basin Finance Journal, 8*(2), 153–175. https://doi.org/10.1016/s0927-538x(00)00009-3

Chen, Y., Liu, M., & Su, J. (2013). Greasing the wheels of bank lending: Evidence from private firms in China. *Journal of Banking & Finance, 37*(7), 2533–2545. https://doi.org/10.1016/j.jbankfin.2013.02.002

Park, J. (2012). Corruption, soundness of the banking sector, and economic growth: A cross-country study. *Journal of International*

Money and Finance, 31(5), 907–929. https://doi.org/10.1016/j.jimonfin.2011.07.007

Dincer, O., & Gunalp, B. (2020). The effects of federal regulations on corruption in U.S. states. *European Journal of Political Economy, 65*, 101924. https://doi.org/10.1016/j.ejpoleco.2020.101924

Rose-Ackerman, S., & Palifka, B. J. (2016). *Corruption and government: Causes, consequences, and reform*. Cambridge University Press.

Deleon, B. (2015, February 25). *Bribes, speed money, extortion, expense reporting fraud*. Bribes, Speed Money, Extortion, Expense Reporting Fraud. Retrieved December 29, 2022, from https://chromeriver.com/blog/bribes-speed-money-extortion-expense-reporting-fraud#:~:text=Also%20known%20as%20%E2%80%9Cgrease%20payments,someone%20should%20be%20doing%20anyway.

Glaeser, E. L., & Saks, R. E. (2006). Corruption in America. *Journal of Public Economics, 90*(6-7), 1053–1072. https://doi.org/10.1016/j.jpubeco.2005.08.007

Charumilind, C., Kali, R., & Wiwattanakantang, Y. (2006). Connected lending: Thailand before the financial crisis*. *The Journal of Business, 79*(1), 181–218. https://doi.org/10.1086/497410

Mohamad, A., & Jenkins, H. (2020). Corruption and banks' non-performing loans: Empirical evidence from MENA countries. *Macroeconomics and Finance in Emerging Market Economies, 14*(3), 308–321. https://doi.org/10.1080/17520843.2020.1842478

Chen, M., Jeon, B. N., Wang, R., & Wu, J. (2015). Corruption and bank risk-taking: Evidence from emerging economies. *Emerging Markets Review, 24*, 122–148. https://doi.org/10.1016/j.ememar.2015.05.009

Nestlé's Scandalous History of Corruption Towards Health In Developed and Developing Nations

Jennifer Nguyen

Background on Corruption in Healthcare

Healthcare systems have been developed and reformed over the past thirty years at an accelerated rate that has significant impacts on lifespan and health outcomes of people today (Durrani, 2016). Such markers include: reduced infant and maternal mortality rates, and global under-5 mortality (Durrani, 2016). Our world population will reach around 9 billion people by 2050 given the revolution in healthcare (Raleigh, 1999). However, equality is yet to be achieved across the world in terms of healthcare financial support. The World Health Organization reported differences among countries for healthcare expenditures, where high income countries had an average estimated USD 3,000 whereas poor countries spent USD 12 (Durrani, 2016). Additionally, many low income countries where poverty and unemployment are endemic experienced a greater burden of communicable and non-communicable diseases (Raleigh, 1999). Some factors that may be pertinent to such stark differences is due to compromised healthcare services, and economic business greed from high income countries. Corruption in the health sector in developing nations, where resources may be constrained, can further exacerbate poor outcomes in citizens. As the healthcare sector may have stakeholders in private sectors, power imbalance and delivery of healthcare services can result in corruption nationally, and in certain cases, on a global scale (United Nations, 2017).

Dr. Patricia García, a researcher and Minister of Health in Peru defines corruption in healthcare as "substantial cost-related driver that affects a programme's sustainability and effectiveness and the possibility of a country's graduation from aid or mother support" in the global context (García, 2019). In clinical settings, David Berger referred to corruption as "kickback that poisons their [doctors' and medical institutions'] integrity and destroys any chance of a trusting relationship with their patients" (Berger, 2014). Necessary medical procedures can be used as a form of economic business greed rather than following patient centered care as outlined by the physician's oath to uphold morality and ethics when practicing medicine (Askitopoulou & Vgontzas, 2018).

With the advent of huge corporations involved with management of resources and finances within the healthcare sector, fraud deeply affects the rights of individuals and communities (National Academies of Sciences, Engineering, and Medicine, 2018). Certain actions can be considered as corruption within healthcare: false marketing to vulnerable populations, exploiting low-income countries for resources and labor, and subverting moral/ethical guidelines set out by international organizations for capital gain. In recent years, Nestlé has made worldwide headlines after class-action lawsuits were filed against them for poor relations practices and misleading advertising, to the detriment of consumers (McNamara, 2022).

The food and drink corporation has been found to abuse human rights and conduct unethical environmental practices to increase sales, violating the World Health Organization Code on multiple occasions

(Mondaq, 2022). The corruption from the companies' various health business ventures meets the criteria of corruption outlined above.

An overview of the breast milk scandal's roots

The Nestlé infant formula scandal is one of the most infamous corporate scandals to ever occur. From the late 1960s to the mid-1980s, Nestlé was accused of unethical marketing practices in the sale of infant formula in developing countries (Boyd, 2012). This scandal not only damaged Nestlé's reputation but also had far-reaching consequences on healthcare in those countries (Lakota People's Law Project, 2021).

The scandal centered around Nestlé's marketing of its infant formula products. The company aggressively marketed its formula to mothers in developing countries, often in areas that lacked access to clean water and proper sanitation facilities (Anttila-Hughes et al., 2018). In order to compete with local breast milk substitutes, Nestlé used tactics such as giving away free formula samples, advertising in health facilities, and even offering free formula to health workers for them to give to mothers. This created a situation where mothers were more likely to use infant formula as a substitute for their own breast milk (Anttila-Hughes et al., 2018).

Negative Health Effects Associated with the Infant Formula Scandal

The use of infant formula was first introduced by Henri Nestle in 1860 for Swiss working-class mothers who could not or did not have time to breastfeed (Schuman, 2003). The product was used in many developing countries to help decrease malnutrition in children and decrease the incidence of low-birth weight infants through Nestlé's prevailing marketing campaigns to keep families reliant on their product (Sri, 2008).

However, using infant formula as a substitute for breast milk comes with significant health risks. According to the World Health Organization, it can lead to higher rates of malnutrition, gastrointestinal infections, diarrhea, and even death in infants (World Health Organization, 2021). This is due to the fact that formula can be contaminated without proper sanitation or clean water, and that breast milk provides nutrition and immunological benefits that formula cannot replicate (Martin et al., 2016). There is scientific evidence that early supplementation of milk formula increases the risk of infection in infants, and alters their gut microbiota towards proliferation of antibiotic-resistant bacteria (Pärnänen et al., 2021).

The Nestlé scandal had a devastating effect on healthcare in the countries where it was practiced. The increased use of formula as a substitute for breast milk resulted in higher rates of malnutrition, gastrointestinal infections, and other health problems in infants (Anttila-Hughes et al., 2018). This in turn put a strain on the already-limited healthcare resources in those countries, as health workers had to deal with the consequences of Nestlé's unethical marketing practices.

The promotion of infant formula in developing nations has also been linked to numerous health problems and deaths due to a number of factors. Firstly, the formula is often mixed with contaminated water, which can lead to bacterial infections such as diarrhea and cholera (Tan, 2021). Secondly, the formula is often too expensive for families living in poverty, leading to malnutrition and higher rates of infant mortality (The Multinational Monitor, 1987). Finally, the promotion of formula over breast milk can lead to a decrease in the amount of natural antibodies and vitamins that a baby would receive from breast milk, leading to a weakened immune system and a higher susceptibility to illnesses. The Nestlé breast milk scandal primarily affected developing countries in Africa and Asia, including India, Pakistan, Kenya, Ethiopia, and Algeria.

The scandal also had a lasting impact on Nestlé's reputation. In 1984, the company was forced to revise its marketing practices, and in 1987 it agreed to abide by the WHO's International Code of Marketing of Breast-milk Substitutes. The company has since been more careful in its marketing practices, but the scandal has tarnished its reputation in the eyes of the general public.

The breast milk boycott of 1977

The Nestlé breast milk boycott began in 1977, when a coalition of health workers, women's groups, and religious organizations launched a boycott of Nestlé products over concerns that the company was promoting the use of infant formula over breast milk in developing countries (Johnson & Duckett, 2020). The boycott was launched in response to Nestlé's aggressive marketing strategies, which included giving away free samples of formula to mothers in poor countries, often without providing instructions on how to use the formula safely (Plüss, 2022). This could lead to malnutrition, dehydration, and even death in infants who were not receiving the proper nutrition from their mother's milk. The boycott was successful and eventually led to a revision of Nestlé's marketing practices (Plüss, 2022).

Positive social outcomes from the breast milk scandal

The Nestlé breast milk scandal had far-reaching social effects, including the following:
1. It highlighted the importance of breastfeeding as the best source of nutrition for infants
and young children, and raised awareness about the dangers of relying on powdered milk formula instead (Martin et al., 2018).
2. It raised awareness about the unethical marketing tactics employed by multinational corporations, such as Nestlé, to target developing countries (Kades, 2022). As a result, it sparked a global movement to

protect the health of mothers and their babies from exploitation and corporate greed (Plüss, 2022).

A further topic of discussion is the role of corporations in global health outcomes. Many global health professionals have posed the question of whether it is the responsibility of businesses to look out for the wellbeing of those living in developing countries, given the different health contexts involved (Theisen & Bruckbauer, 2003). As the risk-factor and burden of diseases disproportionately affects those living in developed nations, such as malnutrition and unsafe drinking water conditions, it is important to address the consequences of organizations when imposing their presence in health systems in vulnerable populations. From this scandal, there is increased scrutiny of the marketing practices of companies that produce and distribute breast milk substitutes (Wattana, 2016). Consequently, governmental bodies in many countries were prompted to introduce legislation to regulate marketing of breast milk substitutes (Pomeranz & Harris, 2019).

The World Health Organization's (WHO) International Code of Marketing of Breast-milk Substitutes (also known as the "WHO Code") is an international health policy that was adopted in 1981 in response to evidence that the inappropriate promotion of breast-milk substitutes (such as infant formula) was contributing to poorer infant and young child health outcomes in many countries (UNICEF, 2022). The WHO Code sets out a number of principles and requirements to ensure that infant formula, follow-on formula and other breast-milk substitutes are not advertised or promoted to the public, health workers or parents directly or indirectly. The Code also sets out criteria for labeling and packaging of breast-milk substitutes, as well as monitoring and compliance guidelines. The WHO Code has been widely adopted across the world, although implementation and enforcement of the Code varies widely.

The Nestlé infant formula scandal is a clear example of how unethical marketing practices can have a damaging effect on healthcare. The company's aggressive marketing tactics led to higher rates of malnutrition and other health problems in infants in developing countries, and put a strain on already-limited healthcare resources (Martin et al., 2016). For this reason, the scandal serves as a reminder of the importance of ethical marketing practices and the need to ensure that healthcare services are not exploited for corporate gain.

The Nestlé water bottle draining scandal

Nestlé has also been accused of draining water resources from developing nations for the purpose of bottling and selling bottled water (Jaffee & Case, 2018). This has caused a number of environmental and health issues in these countries. In addition, Nestlé has been accused of pricing its bottled water out of the reach of many people in developing countries, making it difficult for them to access safe drinking water. This can have serious implications for the health of people living in these countries, as they may be forced to drink contaminated water which can lead to a range of illnesses (Jaffee & Case, 2018). Furthermore, Nestlé has been accused of exploiting water resources, which can have a severe impact on local ecosystems (Jaffee & Case, 2018).

Nestlé has promoted water bottles in developing nations by providing access to clean, safe drinking water in areas with limited access to it. The company has done this by setting up water treatment and distribution systems, providing water purification systems, and launching water education programs (Nestlé, 2022). In addition, Nestlé has provided thousands of bottles of water for those affected by natural disasters. Nestlé has also partnered with NGOs and other organizations to help bring clean water to developing nations. Unfortunately, it has also been accused of draining water resources from developing nations for their own business practices. This has included drawing water from local sources in countries such as India and Pakistan, where water is already scarce, and depleting aquifers in California. In some cases, the company has been accused of taking water away from local communities who rely on it for their own livelihoods. Nestlé has also faced criticism for its water-intensive bottling operations, which use large amounts of water to produce bottled water (Jaffee & Case, 2018). In response to these criticisms, Nestlé has taken steps to reduce its water consumption, including investing in more efficient technologies and setting up water-saving initiatives.

The India case of water draining

Nestlé has been accused of draining water from India and other countries for its bottled water brands (Business of Human Rights, 2018). The company has been accused of taking water from local water sources and using it for its bottled water operations, leaving local communities without sufficient access to water. This has had a detrimental effect on the health of those communities, with a lack of access to clean water leading to water-borne illnesses and other diseases. Additionally, the loss of water has caused a decrease in crop yields, leading to food insecurity among local communities.

The Pakistan case of water draining

Nestlé has additionally drained water from Pakistan by taking groundwater from the Punjab province for its bottling plants (Business of Human Rights, 2018). This has caused some serious health effects for the local communities, as the water table has been significantly lowered which has caused a shortage of drinking water in some areas. It has also caused an increase in waterborne diseases, due to the water being contaminated by industrial and agricultural runoff. Additionally, the groundwater has been polluted with nitrates and heavy metals, leading to serious health issues for those living close to the bottling plants.

The America case of water draining

Nestlé has been draining water from America's rivers and lakes for its bottled water operations for decades (Business of Human Rights, 2018). This has had serious health effects, including depleting water levels in communities and reducing water quality. This has caused a decrease in fish populations, caused an increase in the cost of drinking water, and depleted water resources around the area. It has also caused a decrease in the water table, which has led to water shortages in some areas. In addition, the bottling process has been linked to the release of pollutants into the water supply.

Nestlé has been draining water from California's Strawberry Creek for years, and the company has come under fire for its activities in the state (Denny, 2021). California is known for its water scarcity problems, and Nestlé has been accused of taking more water than it is legally entitled to. The company has also been criticized for not being transparent about its water usage, leaving many to question how much water Nestlé is really using.

Nestlé first began taking water from Strawberry Creek in the late 1990s, when it purchased a permit to pipe water from the creek to its bottling plant in nearby Sacramento (Denny, 2021). This permit was granted by the California Department of Water Resources (DWR), and it allowed Nestlé to take up to 2.3 million gallons of water a year from the creek.

But in recent years, Nestlé has been taking much more than the 2.3 million gallons it is legally entitled to (Denny, 2021). In 2015, Nestlé was found to be taking up to 4.5 million gallons of water a year from the creek, despite the fact that the creek is prone to drought and is already over-tapped by other water users (Denny, 2021).

Nestlé has been able to get away with taking more water than it is legally entitled to for two main reasons. First, the DWR has been slow to update its regulations to reflect the changing water needs of California. Second, Nestlé has been able to take advantage of loopholes in the regulations, such as the fact that permits are only required for water taken from surface sources such as streams and rivers (California State Water Quality, 2022). Nestlé has apparently been taking water from underground sources and not reporting it, which has allowed it to exceed its permit limits.

The excessive water usage has been having a detrimental impact on Strawberry Creek. The creek is already over-tapped by other water users, and Nestlé's additional water withdrawals have been causing the creek to run dry during the summer months. This has had a severe impact on the local environment, as the creek is home to many species of fish and other wildlife (California State Water Quality, 2022).

Nestlé has come under fire for its activities in California, with environmental groups and local residents accusing the company of exploiting a drought-stricken state for its own commercial gain (California State Water Quality, 2022). The issue has even attracted the attention of the International Joint Commission, an organization that monitors water resources between the United States and Canada (Anishinaabe, 2008). The controversy surrounding Nestlé's activities in California has prompted the company to increase its transparency about the amount of water it is taking from Strawberry Creek. Nestlé has also pledged to reduce its water usage in the area, and it has stated that it has already begun to do so. However, many remain skeptical about Nestlé's commitment to sustainability and are calling for stronger regulations to ensure that the company does not exceed its legal water usage limits (Anishinaabe, 2008).

Conclusion

While the history of Nestlé's corrupt business practices have been well documented and there are organizations fighting against the ethical issues posed, the company still has worldwide reach into many sectors of the food and drink industry, which impacts the health and livelihood of many individuals. The company's commodification of critical resources for profit and extreme lengths of unethical promotion towards vulnerable parents in developing countries must be condemned through governmental legislation and advocacy to stop their exploitative behaviors. Given their for-profit model, the best way to object to Nestlé's corrupt operations is through boycotting their products and affiliated work on a global scale. Furthermore, interventions such as prohibiting doctors/government officials from accepting the benefits that Nestlé may give as incentives can help reduce biases towards their actions. Finally, education is vital for consumers to be aware of the detrimental health effects this can pose on themselves. Especially in low-income countries, where parents may not know of the consequences associated with Nestlé's milk formula, it can be seen as a viable nutrient substitute. However, non-profit organizations working abroad should detail health and nutrition to reduce the infant mortality rates.

References

Anttila-Hughes, J., Fernald, L. C. H., Gertler, P., Krause, P., & Wydick, B. (2018). Mortality from Nestlé's marketing of infant formula in low and middle-income countries. NATIONAL BUREAU OF ECONOMIC RESEARCH. https://doi.org/10.3386/w24452

Askitopoulou, H., & Vgontzas, A. N. (2018). The relevance of the Hippocratic Oath to the ethical and moral values of contemporary medicine. Part II: Interpretation of the Hippocratic Oath-today's perspective. European Spine Journal : Official publication of the European Spine Society, the European Spinal Deformity Society, and the European Section of the Cervical Spine Research Society, 27(7), 1491–1500. https://doi.org/10.1007/s00586-018-5615-z

Berger, D. (2014). Corruption ruins the doctor-patient relationship in India. British Medical Journal, 348(3). https://doi.org/10.1136/bmj.g3169

Boyd, C. (2012). The Nestlé Infant Formula Controversy and a Strange Web of Subsequent Business Scandals. Journal of Business Ethics, 106(3), 283–293. http://www.jstor.org/stable/41426691

Canada: Nestlé allegedly extracting water from indigenous land without consent while local residents lack drinking water. Business & Human Rights Resource Centre. (2018, November 7). Retrieved December 22, 2022, from https://www.business-humanrights.org/en/latest-news/canada-nestl%C3%A9-allegedly-extracting-water-from-indigenous-land-without-consent-while-local-residents-lack-drinking-water/

California State Water Quality Control Board. (2022). Bluetriton Brands (formerly Nestlé) springwater extractions in San Bernardino National Forest. SWRCB.gov. Retrieved December 22, 2022, from https://www.waterboards.ca.gov/waterrights/water_issues/programs/enforcement/complaints/nestle.html

Denny, E. (2021, December 10). California officials move to stop Nestlé from taking millions of gallons of water from public streams. EcoWatch. Retrieved December 22, 2022, from https://www.ecowatch.com/california-nestle-water-public-lands-2652807771.html

Durrani H. (2016). Healthcare and healthcare systems: inspiring progress and future prospects. mHealth, 2, 3. https://doi.org/10.3978/j.issn.2306-9740.2016.01.03

Healthcare among most corrupt sectors, warns UN expert, backing "Citizen whistleblowers".OHCHR. (2017, October 24). Retrieved December 22, 2022, from https://www.ohchr.org/en/press-releases/2017/10/healthcare-among-most-corrupt-sectors-warns-un-expert-backing-citizen

Jaffee, D., & Case, J.A. (2018). Draining us dry: scarcity discourses in contention over bottled water extraction. Local Environment, 23(4), 485-501.https://doi.org/10.1080/13549839.2018.1431616

Johnson, D.A. & Duckett, L.J. (2020). Advocacy, strategy and tactics used to confront corporate power: The Nestle Boycott and international code of marketing of breast-milk substitutes. Journal of Human Lactation, 36(4), 568-578. https://doi.org/10.1177/0890334420955158

Kades, A. (2022, February 23). "deeply troubling" marketing landscape across infant formula,who flags. Nutrition Insight. Retrieved December 22, 2022, from https://www.nutritioninsight.com/news/deeply-troubling-marketing-landscape-across-infant-formula-who-flags.html

Martin, C.R., Ling, P., Blackburn, G.L. (2016). Review of infant feeding: Key features of breast milk and infant formula. Nutrients, 8(5), 279. https://doi.org/10.3390%2Fnu8050279

National Academies of Sciences, Engineering, and Medicine; Health and Medicine Division; Board on Health Care Services; Board on Global Health; Committee on Improving the Quality of Health Care Globally. (2018, August 20). 6 the critical health impacts of corruption. Crossing the Global Quality Chasm: Improving Health Care Worldwide. Retrieved December 22, 2022, from https://www.ncbi.nlm.nih.gov/books/NBK535646/

Nestlé facing class-action false advertising suit over boost glucose control drinks. (2022, November 7). Retrieved December 22, 2022, from https://www.mondaq.com/unitedstates/advertising-marketing-branding/1248314/Nestlé-facing-class-action-false-advertising-suit-over-boost-glucose-control-drinks

Nestlé's latest exploits. Lakota People's Law Project. (2021). Retrieved December 22, 2022, from https://lakotalaw.org/news/2021-01-13/Nestlé-pledge-update

Pärnänen, K. M., Hultman, J., Markkanen, M., Satokari, R., Rautava, S., Lamendella, R., Wright, J., McLimans, C. J., Kelleher, S. L., & Virta, M. P. (2021). Early-life formula feeding is associated with infant gut microbiota alterations and an increased antibiotic resistance load. The American Journal of Clinical Nutrition, 115(2), 407–421. https://doi.org/10.1093/ajcn/nqab353

Plüss, J. D. (2022, February 28). Who slams baby milk industry for rampant 'manipulative' marketing. SWI swissinfo.ch. Retrieved December 22, 2022, from https://www.swissinfo.ch/eng/business/who-slams-baby-milk-industry-for-rampant–manipulative--marketing/47369706

Pomeranz, J. L., & Harris, J. L. (2019). Federal regulation of infant and toddler food and drink marketing and labeling. American Journal of Law & Medicine, 45(1), 32–56. https://doi.org/10.1177/0098858819849991
Raleigh V. S. (1999). World population and health in transition. BMJ (Clinical research ed.),319(7215), 981–984. https://doi.org/10.1136/bmj.319.7215.981

Schuman, A. J. (2003, February 1). A concise history of infant formula (Twists and turns included). Contemporary Pediatrics. Retrieved

December 22, 2022, from https://www.contemporarypediatrics.com/view/concise-history-infant-formula-twists-and-turns-included

Sustainable Water Management in our operations. Nestlé Global. (2022). Retrieved December 22, 2022, from https://www.nestle.com/sustainability/water/sustainable-water-efficiency-operations

Sri, E. (2008). Powdered infant formula in developing and other countries-issues and prospects. Emerging Issues in Food Safety, 221-234. http://dx.doi.org/10.1128/9781555815608.ch8

Tan, M. (2021). Controversy over the regulations of infant milk formula marketing from 1970s to 2000s: An analysis on the use of evidence in health policymaking. Journal of Health Policy and Economics, 1(1). Retrieved December 22, 2022, from https://johpec.lse.ac.uk/articles/39/

The International Code of Marketing of Breastmilk Substitutes. Baby Friendly Initiative. (2022, April 20). Retrieved December 22, 2022, from https://www.unicef.org.uk/babyfriendly/baby-friendly-resources/international-code-marketing-breastmilk-substitutes-resources/the-code/

The Multinational Monitor. (1987, April). Infant formula: Hawking Disaster in the Third World. Corporate Crime and Violence. Retrieved December 22, 2022, from https://multinationalmonitor.org/hyper/issues/1987/04/formula.html

Water pact will deplete Great Lakes, expert fears. Anishinaabe. (2008, July 23). Retrieved December 22, 2022, from https://www.anishinaabe.ca/water-pact-will-deplete-great-lakes-expert-fears/

Wattana, M. (2016). The baby bottle and the bottom line: Corporate strategies and the infant formula controversy in the 1970s. Yale University, History of Science, Medicine and Public Health. Retrieved December 22, 2022, from https://hshm.yale.edu/sites/default/files/files/Wattana%20senior%20essay%202016.pdf

World Health Organization. (n.d.). Infant Nutrition - Global. World Health Organization. Retrieved December 11, 2022, from https://www.who.int/health-topics/infant-nutrition

Corruption in the Pharmaceutical Company

Ivy Truong

Corruption in the pharmaceutical industry can take many forms, including the manipulation of clinical trial data, the over-prescription of drugs for financial gain, and the bribery of doctors and other healthcare professionals. These practices can result in the approval and marketing of drugs that are not effective or safe, and can even cause harm to patients. Notable cases of this are Purdue Pharma, GlaxoSmithKline (GSK), Insys Therapeutics, Allergan, and Novartis, wrecking havoc that can still be felt across the globe.

The international detriment created by Purdue Pharma

The modern-day opioid crisis
In many countries over the past 25 years, doctors have been more inclined to prescribe opioids for chronic pain caused by conditions other than cancer (Rosenblum et al., 2008). A sharp rise in opioid-related mortality has coincided with the growing usage of opioids. The number of deaths involving opioid analgesics in the US grew from 4041 in 1999 to 14459 in 2007 (Foundation, 2022), surpassing mortality from multiple myeloma, HIV, and alcoholic liver disease. Other countries, such as the United Kingdom, have also seen an increase

in the prescribing of opioids and opioid-related deaths, the majority of which are unintentional and involve relatively young people. Despite the lack of widespread access to drug-specific data, oxycodone-related deaths have climbed particularly quickly in a number of jurisdictions, including Ontario in Canada and Victoria in Australia (Rintoul et al., 2010) (Canadian Institute for Health Information, 2019).

Marketing without evidence

Despite the long-standing hesitancy surrounding opioid use, Purdue Pharma was able to push its use to clinicians and patients without sufficient evidence of its efficacy. OxyContin was unveiled by Purdue Pharma in 1995 as a "miracle medication" to treat chronic pain (Chow, 2019). The tablet in OxyContin's extended release formulation would release and dissolve gradually. One dose, according to Purdue Pharma, was supposed to be able to ease pain for the following 12 hours, more than twice as long as the effects of other medications, which only had an effect on pain for 4-6 hours. (Van Zee, 2009) With this assertion, they captured the interest of both patients and physicians by introducing a novel concept in pain management: patients might enjoy a pleasant night without having to get up throughout the night or interrupt their day to take their painkillers. However, Purdue Pharma made numerous untrue statements about the drug's window of pain relief, superiority to alternative treatments, and risk of addiction in the course of marketing and promoting OxyContin.

The authors of one Cochrane study came to the conclusion that there is insufficient evidence to recommend the use of opioids for treating chronic non-cancer pain, even in cases with severe osteoarthritis pain (Dhalla et al., 2011). An observational study that was recently released lends credence to the idea that in this situation, opioids' hazards outweigh their advantages. Because of the scarcity of high-quality evidence, individuals who create clinical practice guidelines are in the unfortunate situation of having insufficient data on which to base important recommendations. As a result, some guidelines just advise doctors to "examine the data relating to effectiveness" before deciding to start treatment, rather than recommending for or against the long-term use of opioids (Dhalla et al., 2011).

Drug manufacturers have aggressively marketed opioids for use in people with persistent non-cancer pain despite the lack of supporting data. Because successful legal actions against Purdue and some of its executives have made public many parts of its marketing, the case of OxyContin, a sustained release version of oxycodone produced by Purdue Pharma in North America, deserves special attention (Van Zee, 2009). Purdue admitted in court documents and during a US Congressional probe that company workers had lied to doctors about the dangers of addiction. Some workers of Purdue advised using OxyContin to "filter out" drug users and addicts, while others profited from the widespread misconception that oxycodone is less effective than morphine when the opposite is true (Dhalla et al., 2011). Given the drug's propensity for abuse and death, some parts of Purdue's marketing strategies stand out in particular. The firm sought out doctors who regularly prescribed OxyContin, offered salespeople generous bonuses to boost OxyContin sales, and distributed coupons that allowed new patients to receive free samples at participating pharmacies (Van Zee, 2009). Other opioid producers have also received criticism for improper marketing. For instance, the US Food and Drug Administration issued a warning to Janssen Pharmaceuticals for making deceptive safety and unsupported effectiveness claims for its transdermal fentanyl patch (U.S. Food & Drug Administration, 2021). Similar to this, the FDA cautioned King Pharmaceuticals that "the concealment of significant and potentially deadly hazards" related to their morphine-naltrexone product was "especially flagrant and disturbing in its potential impact on the public health." (Dhalla et al., 2011).

One of the greatest breakthrough claims of Purdue was the promise of

12-hour pain relief. The 12-hour-relief promise offered a remarkable image of a world in which patients would only require two pills per day to get pain relief. The 12-hour respite promise, however, did not hold true in many situations (Chow, 2019). In Purdue Pharma's own clinical trials, which were carried out in accordance with a potential drug application to the US Food & Drug Administration (FDA) for approval, they reported that many patients who were prescribed OxyContin were asking for more painkillers before their next dose, which was scheduled for 12 hours later (Chow, 2019). Many patients were either switched to OxyContin dosages that lasted for eight hours or taken additional medicines in between the two OxyContin doses. Purdue Pharma continued to push for FDA approval of OxyContin as an analgesic that provides 12 hours of relief despite the knowledge that the 12-hour-relief claim was untrue for many patients (Chow, 2019). The company then produced lengthy advertisements in medical journals to unequivocally state that effective pain relief in patients can be achieved by a 12-hour dosage regimen (Van Zee, 2009). Even while Purdue Pharma's lawyers acknowledged in a 2004 letter to the FDA that 8-hour dosages could improve patient care, they claimed that a 12-hour window of pain relief was better for business since it painted OxyContin in a more favourable light than alternative treatments (Ryan et al., 2016).

Another false claim is that OxyContin was greatly superior to pre-existing treatments and painkillers. Purdue Pharma stated that OxyContin is superior to several existing treatments, such as the hydrocodone and acetaminophen combo therapy, in advertising materials for the drug (Chakradhar & Ross, 2019). Clinical trials, however, did not demonstrate that OxyContin was better than currently available therapies; rather, they simply demonstrated that it was similar to them (Van Zee, 2009). Similar efficacy and safety were observed in randomised controlled trials comparing the new "wonder medication" with extended-release formula to the existing immediate-release oxycodone, which is delivered four times per day. In randomised controlled studies, OxyContin was also compared to morphine and found to have similar efficacy and safety profiles (Heiskanen & Kalso, 1997). Although OxyContin has a similar analgesic profile to other medications, Purdue Pharma promoted OxyContin as being more effective than some other treatments. As a result, the FDA issued written warnings to Purdue Pharma regarding these false marketing claims (Chakradhar & Ross, 2019).

The last major, and arguably the most damaging claim was the claim that OxyContin was non-addictive, despite the long history of fighting against opioid (ex. China's Opioid Crisis) and the deep-rooted fear of opioid addiction. When writing in their advertising materials that the danger of addiction to OxyContin was modest and when teaching their sales personnel to advertise that the risk of addiction was less than 1%, Purdue Pharma misrepresented the risk of addiction as being low (Chow, 2019). However, in actuality, the risk of addiction among Purdue Pharma's target market of patients with chronic, non-cancer pain might be as high as 50% , with numerous studies indicating that 20–40% of individuals abuse prescription drugs (Chabal et al., 1997).

Marketing tactics

In hindsight, it appears ridiculous that such outrageous claims were believed by not just the American population, but also clinicians as well. Despite the unfounded assertions and public data to the contrary, OxyContin's sales soared from $48 million in 1996 to $1.1 billion in 2000 to $3 billion in 2010 despite the negative press (Van Zee, 2009). The prescription medicine sales for OxyContin generated nearly ten times more income than MS Contin, the company's previous top-selling medication (Van Zee, 2009). Purdue Pharma spent a large amount on intensive marketing and promotion initiatives that resulted in the successful commercialization of OxyContin. Their marketing spend was significantly higher than what they had previously spent on MS Contin and significantly higher than that of competitors of OxyContin, such as

Duragesic from Janssen Pharmaceuticals (Chow, 2019). They engaged in extensive and unprecedented marketing campaigns targeted largely at physicians with their much greater budget in order to boost the number of prescriptions for OxyContin.

While Purdue Pharma is supposedly a pharmaceutical company, spending and focus was primarily on the sales team. Purdue Pharma increased its sales staff to over 600 sales reps when OxyContin was introduced, investing more than $200 million in the expansion (Van Zee, 2009). Then, Purdue Pharma trained their sales people to persuade doctors to prescribe OxyContin for a variety of common pain ailments while fraudulently assuring them of the drug's low risk of addiction. Purdue Pharma then used prescription profiles of individual doctors to identify doctors who are the biggest opioid prescribers, and they deployed its sales representatives to persuade those doctors to prescribe OxyContin in order to maximise the influence of their massive sales team. A highly motivated sales force that stood to gain significantly from a generous bonus structure based on sales volume was the key to Purdue Pharma's aggressive marketing strategies' ultimate success. Sales reps were encouraged to support higher dose strengths since they were rewarded with bonuses if more of their prescribers used high doses of OxyContin.

Further, Purdue Pharma was able to rope in doctors to prescribe OxyContin at great ease, despite it being an opioid. Purdue Pharma gave clinicians freebies in kind, subtly influencing how they write prescriptions. Numerous pain management symposiums were conducted by them across the country, and thousands of doctors, pharmacists, and nurses were given free trips to attend them; it has been suggested that these sponsored excursions influenced how often clinicians prescribed OxyContin (Orlowski & Wateska, 1992). Sales agents also sent promotional items with the OxyContin brand, including fishing hats, plush toys, and baggage tags, to serve as a reminder for healthcare professionals about OxyContin (Patrick Radden Keefe, 2017). The aggressive marketing strategy employed by Purdue Pharma was ultimately responsible for the drug's economic success and high income. OxyContin became the most often prescribed brand-name opioid in the US for the treatment of moderate to severe pain in the early 2000s.

Changes in the aftermath

Decades after the release of OxyContin, when the societal effects and the corrupt intentions of Purdue Pharma could no longer be denied, changes were made to regulate pharmaceutical companies. The involvement of multiple systems and institutions meant widespread sweep and changes must be made. Because of the breakdown of the current infrastructure as well as the inadequacy of the infrastructure, fraudulent claims in marketing materials have flourished. The FDA is given the power by the Food, Medicine, and Cosmetics Acts to control prescription drug advertising and promotion and to guarantee that such activity is honest. However, the FDA's 39 employees were overburdened during Purdue Pharma's marketing campaign with the revision of 34,000 promotional packets; it was very challenging for the FDA's small team to carefully examine each promotional package in a timely manner and safeguard the public from fraudulent claims (Chow, 2019). The Food, Drug and Cosmetics Act's requirement was not carried out by the FDA because of its overburdened staff. The FDA marketing approval mechanism was more similar to a post-marketing warning to the FDA than a pre-market approval system (Chow, 2019). Consequently, it was insufficient in stopping the spread of Purdue Pharma's misleading claims. The FDA was only required to assess promotional materials once they were submitted for approval, not before they were used, as required by regulation (Van Zee, 2009). Therefore, even if the FDA can evaluate marketing materials promptly, the marketing materials would already have reached doctors and the public before the FDA took any action to stop further marketing.

The role of clinicians in creating the opioid epidemic was also undeniable. Despite their lack of bad intentions, their obliviousness to the dangers of OxyContin and their failure to uphold their position as healthcare providers implicates them. Purdue Pharma's marketing strategy was effective and harmful to public health because of its close relationships and power over practitioners. Particularly, the in-kind gifts given to medical professionals influenced how they treated patients, maybe as a result of a lack of regulation in this area. Even though professional organisations like the American Medical Association have taken positive steps to encourage doctors not to accept sizable gifts from the pharmaceutical business, an advice system is not as effective as one that is regulated (*Gifts to Physicians from Industry*, 2020). A regulatory mechanism might be created and put in place so that clinicians must inform their licencing or regulating body of any connections to the pharmaceutical business and obtain permission before working with it (Orlowski & Wateska, 1992). Similar to the suggestion to convert the FDA to a pre-market notice system, this will probably require a sizable budget and staff (Chow, 2019).

Bribery by GlaxoSmithKline

The Justice Department announced today that the largest pharmaceutical company in the world, GlaxoSmithKline LLC (GSK), has agreed to plead guilty and pay $3 billion to resolve its criminal and civil liability related to the company's illegal promotion of certain prescription drugs, its failure to report certain safety data, and its civil liability for alleged false price reporting practises. The settlement is both the largest payout ever made by a pharma firm and the largest health care fraud settlement in American history (Office of Public Affairs, 2012).

GSK consented to enter a guilty plea to a three-count criminal information, which included two counts of selling Paxil and Wellbutrin under false pretences in interstate commerce and one count of failing to alert the Food and Medicine Administration of safety information regarding the drug Avandia (FDA) (Office of Public Affairs, 2012). According to the terms of the plea deal, GSK will lose $43,185,600 in addition to paying a total of $1 billion in restitution, which includes a $956,814,400 criminal penalty (Office of Public Affairs, 2012). The criminal plea agreement also calls for the president and board of directors of GSK in the United States to make a number of non-financial compliance undertakings. GSK's guilty plea and punishment aren't official unless the U.S. District Court accepts them. In order to satisfy its civil obligations to the federal government and the states under the False Claims Act, GSK will also pay $2 billion. In addition to resolving pricing fraud charges, the civil settlement resolves claims involving Paxil, Wellbutrin, Avandia, and other medications (Office of Public Affairs, 2012).

The arrangement with GSK covers a number of its top medications. Even though the Food and Drug Administration had never approved paroxetine for use in treating patients under the age of 18, it was nonetheless illegally promoted for that purpose (Office of Public Affairs, 2012). The corporation allegedly published "misleading" journal publications asserting the effectiveness of paroxetine in that population when, according to the Justice Department's statement, "the study failed to demonstrate efficacy." It also concealed trials that had unfavourable results (Office of Public Affairs, 2012).

GSK illegally advertised bupropion for attention-deficit/hyperactivity disorder, weight loss, sexual dysfunction, drug addiction, and other off-label applications. Additionally, extravagant travel incentives, "false advisory boards, and apparently impartial continuing medical education (CME) programmes" were used to promote illegal drug use (Office of Public Affairs, 2012).

Ondansetron, which is only approved for postoperative nausea, the anticonvulsant lamotrigine, and the anti-asthma medication fluticasone were also encouraged for usage off-label (Roehr, 2012). Healthcare professionals received kickbacks for dispensing these and other medications. Federal health insurance programmes like Medicare and Medicaid were fraudulently used as a result (Roehr, 2012).

Keeping trial outcomes secret
Eliot Spitzer, the attorney general of New York state, launched a civil lawsuit accusing the drug company of "repeated and persistent fraud" for allegedly hiding the findings of research that revealed paroxetine was unsuccessful in treating adolescent depression.

Five studies in particular have received a lot of attention. In two of them, depressed teenagers who received paroxetine instead of a placebo exhibited no improvement. Even though there were no actual suicides, three of the patients showed signs of an increase in suicidal behaviour and ideation (Nevels et al., 2016). According to a 1998 internal SmithKline Beecham memo that Mr. Spitzer possesses, it would be commercially unacceptable to acknowledge that paroxetine was ineffective in youngsters. In order to minimise any potential negative effects, the corporation would need to properly regulate the spread of these data (Dyer, 2004).

After a decade of increased antidepressant use among youths, Paroxetine received more attention in the early 2000s due to worries regarding a connection between paroxetine and child suicidality. The extent of GSK's dedication to complete transparency is being put to the test by one group's request for data. The findings of study 329 in particular, a trial run of Paroxetine for the treatment of depression in teenagers (Le Noury et al., 2015). The internal report GSK published on study 329 is incomplete, missing an unknown number of pages that contain original case report forms.

Conclusion

This resolution represents a step in the direction of the Health Care Fraud Prevention and Enforcement Action Team (HEAT) project, which was launched in May 2009 by Attorney General Eric Holder and Secretary of Health and Human Services Kathleen Sebelius (Office of Public Affairs, 2012). Through improved collaboration, the two departments' alliance has concentrated efforts on reducing and preventing Medicare and Medicaid financial fraud. With regard to health care fraud cases pursued under the False Claims Act and the Food, Drug, and Cosmetic Act, the department has recovered a total of more than $10.2 billion in settlements, verdicts, fines, restitution, and forfeiture over the last three years (Office of Public Affairs, 2012).

Conclusion

Pharmaceutical firms Purdue Pharma and GlaxoSmithKline have both been charged with corruption in the past. The marketing and sales of the highly addictive opioid painkiller OxyContin by Purdue Pharma, which helped fuel the country's opioid crisis, have drawn harsh criticism. The business and its owners, the Sackler family, have also been charged with engaging in dishonest and misleading marketing strategies and neglecting the dangers of OxyContin addiction.

On the other hand, GlaxoSmithKline has been charged with paying bribes to doctors and government representatives in order to promote its medications and boost sales. Additionally, the business has been charged with concealing unfavourable information regarding its medications and participating in other fraudulent practices.

Unethical and even criminal action by both GlaxoSmithKline and Purdue Pharma has had major negative effects on the public. Pharmaceutical businesses must be held responsible for their activities and put the safety and welfare of their clients ahead of their bottom line.

References

Canadian Institute for Health Information. (2019). *Opioid Prescribing in Canada: How Are Practices Changing?* (T. Gomes & B. Sproule, Eds.). Canadian Institute for Health Information.

Chabal, C., Erjavec, M. K., Jacobson, L., Mariano, A., & Chaney, E. (1997). Prescription opiate abuse in chronic pain patients: clinical criteria, incidence, and predictors. *The Clinical Journal of Pain*, *13*(2), 150–155. https://doi.org/10.1097/00002508-199706000-00009

Chakradhar, S., & Ross, C. (2019, December 3). *The history of OxyContin, told through Purdue Pharma documents*. STAT. https://www.statnews.com/2019/12/03/oxycontin-history-told-through-purdue-pharma-documents/

Chow, R. (2019). Purdue Pharma and OxyContin – A Commercial Success But a Public Health Disaster. *HPHR Journal*, *25*. https://doi.org/10.54111/0001/y5

Dhalla, I. A., Persaud, N., & Juurlink, D. N. (2011). Facing up to the prescription opioid crisis. *British Medical Journal*, *343*(7823), 569–571. https://doi.org/10.1136/bmj.d5142

Dyer, O. (2004). GlaxoSmithKline faces US lawsuit over concealment of trial results. *British Medical Journal*, *328*(7453), 1395. https://doi.org/10.1136/bmj.328.7453.1395

Foundation, R. R. (2022, November 16). *Causes of Death in the United States*. Drug Policy Facts. https://www.drugpolicyfacts.org/chapter/causes_of_death#:~:text=%22From%201999%20to%202007%2C%20the

Gifts to Physicians from Industry. (2020). American Medical Association. https://code-medical-ethics.ama-assn.org/ethics-opinions/gifts-physicians-industry

Heiskanen, T., & Kalso, E. (1997). Controlled-release oxycodone and morphine in cancer related pain. *PAIN*, *73*(1), 37–45. https://doi.org/10.1016/s0304-3959(97)00072-9

Højsted, J., & Sjøgren, P. (2007). Addiction to opioids in chronic pain patients: A literature review. *European Journal of Pain*, *11*(5), 490–518. https://doi.org/10.1016/j.ejpain.2006.08.004

Le Noury, J., Nardo, J. M., Healy, D., Jureidini, J., Raven, M., Tufanaru, C., & Abi-Jaoude, E. (2015). Restoring Study 329: efficacy and harms of paroxetine and imipramine in treatment of major depression in adolescence. *British Medical Journal*, *351*. https://doi.org/10.1136/bmj.h4320

Nevels, R. M., Gontkovsky, S. T., & Williams, B. E. (2016). Paroxetine- The Antidepressant from Hell? Probably Not, But Caution Required. *Psychopharmacology Bulletin*, *46*(1), 77–104. https://www.ncbi.nlm.nih.gov/pmc/articles/PMC5044489/

Office of Public Affairs. (2012, July 2). *GlaxoSmithKline to Plead Guilty and Pay $3 Billion to Resolve Fraud Allegations and Failure to Report Safety Data*. The United States Department of Justice. https://www.justice.gov/opa/pr/glaxosmithkline-plead-guilty-and-pay-3-billion-resolve-fraud-allegations-and-failure-report

Orlowski, J. P., & Wateska, L. (1992). The Effects of Pharmaceutical Firm Enticements on Physician Prescribing Patterns. *Chest*, *102*(1), 270–273. https://doi.org/10.1378/chest.102.1.270

Patrick Radden Keefe. (2017, October 23). *The Family That Built an Empire of Pain*. The New Yorker. https://www.newyorker.com/magazine/2017/10/30/the-family-that-built-an-empire-of-pain

Rintoul, A. C., Dobbin, M. D. H., Drummer, O. H., & Ozanne-Smith, J. (2010). Increasing deaths involving oxycodone, Victoria, Australia, 2000-09. *Injury Prevention, 17*(4), 254–259. https://doi.org/10.1136/ip.2010.029611

Roehr, B. (2012). GlaxoSmithKline is fined record $3bn in US. *British Medical Journal, 345*(7864), 2. https://doi.org/10.1136/bmj.e4568

Rosenblum, A., Marsch, L. A., Joseph, H., & Portenoy, R. K. (2008). Opioids and the treatment of chronic pain: Controversies, current status, and future directions. *Experimental and Clinical Psychopharmacology, 16*(5), 405–416. https://doi.org/10.1037/a0013628

Ryan, H., Girion, L., & Glover, S. (2016, May 5). *"You want a description of hell?" OxyContin's 12-hour problem*. LA Times. https://www.latimes.com/projects/oxycontin-part1/

U.S. Food & Drug Administration. (2021 21). *Accidental Exposures to Fentanyl Patches Continue to Be Deadly to Children*. FDA. https://www.fda.gov/consumers/consumer-updates/accidental-exposures-fentanyl-patches-continue-be-deadly-children

Van Zee, A. (2009). The Promotion and Marketing of OxyContin: Commercial Triumph, Public Health Tragedy. *American Journal of Public Health, 99*(2), 221–227. https://doi.org/10.2105/ajph.2007.131714

The Impact of Corruption on Canada's Indigenous Community

Maria Ivanova

Introduction

Long before Frenchman Jacques Cartier entered Canada in 1534, it was already inhabited by a diverse group of First Nations people who referred to their land as "Kanata", meaning "village". Archaeological evidence has shown that First Nations occupied North America for at least 12,000 years before European explorers first arrived (Defence, 2018). The First Nations at the time were divided into 6 groups: Woodland, Iroquoian, Plains, Plateau, Pacific Coast, and the First Nations of the Mackenzie and Yukon River Basins (*First Nations in Canada*, 2011). The groups were categorized according to the different locations they inhabited and shared a similar way of life that emphasized living off the land and appreciating the natural world. It was tradition for First Nations to hunt and gather plants for food and medicinal purposes, and their diet depended on what was available in their local area (*First Nations in Canada*, 2011). For example, salmon was the primary food source for the Plateau First Nations whereas the Plains First Nations commonly hunted local buffalo (*First Nations in Canada*, 2011).

The First Nations had successfully built a rich and vibrant culture with specific housing, transportation, clothing, and spiritual beliefs, until the invasion by European colonial settlements. The wealth of resources available in Canada was of special interest to the colonizers, and what began as an amicable relationship between the native people and colonizers, eventually became troublesome. Settlers began to demand more property and issued military threats in order to occupy the land they wanted. Eventually, the First Nations surrendered a great deal of their land, losing access to their hunting grounds, and were subject to religious missions attempting to convert them to Christianity (*First Nations in Canada*, 2011). The *Indian Act* was introduced in 1876 and aimed to eliminate First Nation's culture in order to force their assimilation into "superior" British society and culture (*Indian Act | The Canadian Encyclopedia*, n.d.). Seven years after the establishment of the *Indian Act,* the British implemented the residential school system as a method to civilize and assimilate First Nations children (*Indian Act | The Canadian Encyclopedia*, n.d.). This chapter will outline the many ways in which corruption has plagued Canada's Indigenous community beginning with one of the most shameful parts of Canadian history, the residential school system. Additionally, economic disparities between Indigenous and non-Indigenous citizens will be discussed, as well as the corruption by illegal exploitation of land and natural resources in Indigenous communities. Finally, we will conclude with a brief description of instances of overpayment to senior members of the Indigenous government system. For the remainder of this chapter Indigenous peoples will be used as a collective name for the original people of North America as well as their descendants. Presently, the Canadian Constitution recognizes 3 groups of Indigenous peoples: First Nations, Inuit, and Métis (*Indigenous Peoples and Communities*, 2022). According to the 2016 Census, more than 1.67 million individuals in Canada identify themselves as Indigenous (*Indigenous Peoples and Communities*, 2022). Worldwide, there are 476 million Indigenous people who account for 6% of the global population (*Indigenous Peoples*, 2022).

The residential school system and other corrupt policies

Corruption, for the purpose of this chapter, will be defined as "abuse of entrusted power for private gain" (*Corruption and First Nations in Canada*, n.d.) One of the main catalysts for corruption in the Indigenous community was the introduction of the residential school system introduced by the Canadian government. The structure of the residential school system and its introduction are incredibly nuanced, as such, this chapter will only briefly describe the components and ramifications of this system. Residential schools were opened and funded by the Canadian government from 1870-1996, and it is estimated that over 150,000 Indigenous children attended these institutions (Restoule, 2013). The purpose of the schools was to "civilize" the Indigenous children by indoctrinating them into Euro-Canadian and Christian ways of living (Restoule, 2013). To claim that the experiences of the children were negative would be a severe understatement of the magnitude of the situation. Some of the children's common experiences have been documented and include a prohibition on speaking Aboriginal languages, required adoption of the religious denomination of the school, lack of nutritious diet, and segregation based on gender with siblings being unable to contact each other (Restoule, 2013). Case studies have also documented instances of sexual assault, forced abortions and sterilizations, withholding of medical attention, exposure to contagious illnesses, as well as the vilification of cultural traditions, and the use of racist language to address students (Restoule, 2013). These rules were strictly enforced by staff through various forms of abuse such as inserting needles into tongues if children spoke their native language, beating with fists, starvation, and even sexual abuse (Restoule, 2013). As the majority of these children were 4-16 years old and at a critical point of development, these traumatic experienced have had a major impact on overall well-being and development. The effects have been substantial for survivors, as well as their descendants who may now experience the effects of intergenerational trauma through a loss of language, culture, and traditional teachings.

While some may view the monstrosities that occurred within the residential school system as part of a distant past, corrupt policies continue to infiltrate the Indigenous communities of Canada. For example, coerced sterilization, the practice of sterilizing women without free and informed consent, was passed as a law in Canada and not repealed until the 1970s (Leason, 2021). The *Sexual Sterilization Act* allowed for a board to order sterilization if a woman was expected to bear a child who may have a "serious mental disease or mental deficiency" (Dyck, 2013). This law disproportionately targeted Indigenous women as 74% who were presented to the board were eventually sterilized compared to 60% of all patients presented (Leason, 2021). At the time, in Alberta, Indigenous people represented 2.5% of the population but made up 25% of those who were sterilized (Rutherford, 2022). Even though Canada repealed this law, Indigenous women have reported forced sterilization practices as late as 2018 (Zingel, 2019). Another example of a corrupt system was referred to as The Sixties Scoop, where Indigenous children were disproportionately targeted and removed from their families, and placed into the child welfare system (Hanson, n.d.) This unethical removal resulted in one-third of all children in foster care being Indigenous (Hanson, n.d.). Legislation has been placed in an attempt to avoid the disastrous effects of the Sixties Scoop; however, literature has shown that modern child welfare systems continue to disproportionately apprehend Indigenous children into foster homes, this is now being referred to as The Millennium Scoop (Hanson, n.d.). While the government is attempting to make reparations for the damage they have caused to Indigenous individuals, corrupt policies continue to exist, and disproportionate targeting remains.

Ongoing corruption

Many alarming statistics have been revealed within Canada's Indigenous communities as a result of corruption. For instance, Indigenous peoples in Canada experience the highest level of poverty as 1 in 4 adults and 4 in 10 children live in poverty (*Poverty in Canada*, n.d.). Another result of colonial practices and corruption has been an unimaginable rise in the prevalence of homelessness amongst Canada's Indigenous population. Studies have shown that in Toronto, Canada's largest urban centre, Indigenous individuals constitute 15% of those experiencing homelessness, even though they make up only 0.5% of the total population (*Indigenous Peoples | The Homeless Hub*, n.d.). In Northern cities such as Yellowknife or Whitehorse, Indigenous peoples make up a staggering 90% of the homeless population (*Indigenous Peoples | The Homeless Hub*, n.d.). Indigenous youth were also found to have a disproportionately increased prevalence of tobacco and alcohol use when compared to non-Indigenous youth. For example, Indigenous youth were found to be 5.26 times more likely to smoke tobacco, 1.43 times more likely to use alcohol, and 3.42 times more likely to use marijuana (P. H. A. of Canada, 2021). These socioeconomic disadvantages are predicted to contribute to an overall lower average life expectancy for Indigenous peoples when compared to non-Indigenous individuals in Canada. For instance, the life expectancy for males is 8.1 years lower, and for females 5.5 years lower than the rest of the Canadian population (United Nations, 2009). These startling figures have complicated, various causes, yet one factor may be used to enhance our understanding: *corruption*.

Corruption resulting in economic disadvantages

First, it is important to establish why the Indigenous community specifically is vulnerable to corruption. As previously mentioned, Indigenous individuals are more likely to experience poverty, homelessness, and drug and alcohol abuse. As a result of colonialism,

Indigenous individuals remain one of the most marginalized communities in Canada. Studies have shown that in 2006, the median income for Indigenous individuals was 30% lower than the rest of Canadians(Wilson & Macdonald, 2010). This disparity remains whether statistics are withdrawn from rural or urban reserves, as non-Indigenous people working on urban reserves earn 34% more than Indigenous workers, and on rural reserves, non-Indigenous individuals earn a staggering 88% more than Indigenous colleagues (Wilson & Macdonald, 2010). There are many hypotheses regarding the causes of Indigenous poverty, all of which seem to stem from the consequences of colonialism and corruption. For example, the displacement and relocation of Indigenous peoples from resource-rich land disrupted traditional economies and forced individuals to become vulnerable and dependent on the Canadian government (*Poverty and Child Welfare: Poverty in Indigenous and Racialized Communities*, n.d.). Additionally, chronic underfunding and lack of investment in on-reserve services have also been shown to perpetuate poverty in the Indigenous community (*Poverty and Child Welfare: Poverty in Indigenous and Racialized Communities*, n.d.). Further, the cost of living in remote Indigenous communities has soared exponentially in recent years, thus contributing to lower overall disposable income. For remote Indigenous communities, food prices are listed at 2.5 times higher than the national average (Baptiste, 2022). According to Statistics Canada, grocery prices are up nearly 9%, translating to a 20% increase in Indigenous communities and perpetuating even greater financial difficulties in the Indigenous communities (Baptiste, 2022). Several studies have shown a correlation between low-income levels, and a more pronounced experience with corruption (Chêne, 2010). Additionally, as a disadvantaged group, it has been shown that Indigenous peoples have less access to decision-makers, and fewer opportunities to assert their voice regarding their rights and entitlements, thus making them easier targets for corruption (Chêne, 2010). Corruption has also been tied to limiting high-quality education, further compromising low-income individuals earning capacity and economic empowerment (Chêne, 2010).

Corruption as a result of illegal exploitation of land and natural resources

Exploiting the land and natural resources of Indigenous communities is a method of corruption that has far-reaching impacts, many of which are difficult to quantify. The impact of this exploitation can be summed up in one quote that was said in a meeting between two First Nation chiefs. Upon discussing good and bad news, one chief said to the other: "The bad news is that De Beers [diamond mining company] have just discovered diamonds near Attawapiskat [First Nation's location]" (Parlee, 2015). The discovery of diamonds should have been an exciting day for the Indigenous community; however, due to the patterns seen by businesses and the Canadian government, this day only foreshadowed that more exploitation is to come. Indigenous peoples have been shown to have a significant historical attachment to their territories. In their worldview, they preserve their land base in order to protect their culture and maintain the survival of their community, and this is integral to their identity (Hand, 2005). An example of this dedicated devotion to ancestral land was seen when the Sioux tribe refused to accept a $400 million settlement for the Black Hills, the land where the Sioux people originated (Hand, 2005). Despite being low-income, the Sioux people have insisted on reclaiming these hills as they contain the tribe's sacred sites, legendary landmarks, and material resources that sustain the Sioux peoples (Hand, 2005). As Indigenous identity is often tied to the land that they originated from any form of corrupt exploitation of land and resources proves to be extremely detrimental both financially and culturally. As Indigenous communities usually exist on natural resource-rich land, they are often the subject of corrupt dealings and rent-seeking behaviours (Chêne, 2010). This concept is referred to by scholars as the resource curse, wherein an inverse relationship exists between resource abundance and economic growth (Parlee, 2015). The corrupt processes of the Canadian government overtaking Indigenous land have been cited in many instances throughout history. Dating back to 1885, the US government claimed to be a protector of First Nations rights and divided up land held collectively by tribes to individual Indigenous peoples as the government believed individual ownership of land was superior to collective ownership (Hand, 2005). In this process, the government distributed land ownership to select Indigenous individuals and left a "surplus" of land to sell off to non-Indigenous individuals (Hand, 2005). The end result left Indigenous tribes owning 48 acres in the 1930s, compared to the 138 million acres they owned previously (Hand, 2005). More recent examples exist, such as the Athabasca oil sands project (AOSP). The Athabasca oil deposit is located in Alberta and production from this area currently results in over two million barrels of oil per day, with production expected to increase in the coming decades (Parlee, 2015). The land these oil sands are located on is partly on First Nations and Métis reserves, which rely on the ecosystem of the Athabasca oil sands for sustenance, livelihood, and cultural traditions. Unfortunately, oil sand mining has largely restricted their access to this land and its resources (Parlee, 2015). In addition to restricted access, mining practices have also resulted in questionable consequences to the human health of local Indigenous communities. One elder at an Indigenous reserve near the Athabasca oil sands claims, "Oil sands development in the Athabasca region has had devastating effects on our people. We are afraid to drink the water or eat the fish from the river as we have always done. The fish have strange tumors, and cancer rates in our community have increased dramatically in the last 10 years" (Parlee, 2015). Indigenous groups' ability to develop has been limited by the unethical practices of exploitation of land and natural resources.

Corruption as a result of Indigenous governance practices

There have been many instances of corruption noted within the governing bodies of Canadian Indigenous communities. One major theme that has been noted several times in the media is the overpayment of select officeholders. For example, in 2013, Ron Giesbrecht, a Canadian Indigenous leader was paid nearly $1 million while leading a community of 82 individuals (Hopkins, 2014). This number was startling for the community, as Andrea Richer, a spokeswoman for Aboriginal Affairs elaborated "Our government expects First Nation band councils to use taxpayer dollars responsibly and for the benefit of all community members" (Hopkins, 2014). Many of these corrupt practices may arise as conflict-of-interest legislation does not apply to First Nations governments, and as such individuals may simultaneously hold multiple jobs in the government (Flanagan, 2017). For example, Ron Giesbrecht was a British Columbia chief as well as the economic development officer, which allowed him to broker a business deal in his favour that resulted in his elevated salary (Flanagan, 2017). Furthermore, corruption may be seen in the varied salary range for different chiefs which range from $0 to $914,219 (Flanagan, 2017). The upper end of this range goes far beyond the salaries received in municipalities, as well as the provincial and federal governments in the rest of Canada. As Indigenous communities are among some of the most marginalized and low-income members of Canada, their senior members being some of the wealthiest may point to corruption within their governing structures. Unfortunately, elevated compensation has not been shown to correlate with better governance outcomes (Flanagan, 2017). Studies have shown that the most successful Indigenous governments allocate less per capita for compensation of the chief (Flanagan, 2017). While these elevated levels of compensation may not be illegal, they point to corrupt practices wherein select officeholders have disproportionately high incomes when compared to the rest of their community, and non-Indigenous government workers in similar positions. RoseAnne Archibald, a politician and the National Chief of the Assembly of First Nations (AFN) has also elucidated that corrupt government systems may exist within the First Nations. In 2022, she alleged that the AFN which represents First Nations citizens in Canada hid an irregular financial transaction where an employee transferred nearly $200,00 in AFN cash to their personal bank account (Forester, 2022). This employee was paid a retirement payout yet signed a new contract and continued to work full-time. She has since claimed that financial corruption exists inside the AFN, whose job is to appropriately advocate on behalf of First Nations in Canada, and has referred to it as "crooked" (Forester, 2022).

In conclusion, dishonest behaviour has led to several instances of corruption within the Indigenous community. Initially, corruption was seen when the Canadian government enforced attendance at residential schools with the goal of "assimilating" Indigenous children into Euro-Canadian culture. The aftermath of these institutions is an appalling part of Canadian history that has created endless intergenerational trauma within Indigenous communities. Some of the aftermaths of this corruption include a disproportionately low income in Indigenous communities, as well as unequal access to education, increased rates of homelessness, and drug and alcohol abuse. Additionally, the exploitation of land and natural resources by the Canadian government as well as private businesses is yet another instance of the corruption implanted within Indigenous communities. Finally, several instances have revealed a disproportionately elevated salary of senior Indigenous council members, that has not been fairly explained to community members. The Indigenous peoples of Canada have faced obstacles in their quest to reclaim their once-vibrant cultures and means of subsistence as a result of the confluence of these corrupt events. While the past should never be forgotten, Canada has begun to make reparations in order to reconcile their past mistreatment of the Indigenous community. For instance, in 2022, the largest settlement in Canada's history was made, when the Canadian government agreed to pay $31.5 billion to fix the nation's discriminatory child welfare system and compensate children who were unnecessarily removed from their homes, as well as their families (Porter & Isai, 2022). There are still many important steps that must be taken to lessen the effects of corruption, and the Canadian government and its citizens must work tirelessly in order to ensure this objective is met.

References

Baptiste, Z. (2022, May 24). *Rising food prices: How Indigenous communities are responding*. Canadian Feed The Children. https://canadianfeedthechildren.ca/the-feed/food-prices-2022/

Canada, P. H. A. of. (2021, August 23). *Original quantitative research – Tobacco, alcohol and marijuana use among Indigenous youth attending off-reserve schools in Canada: Cross-sectional results from the Canadian Student Tobacco, Alcohol and Drugs Survey* [Research]. https://www.canada.ca/en/public-health/services/reports-publications/health-promotion-chronic-disease-prevention-canada-research-policy-practice/vol-39-no-6-7-2019/tobacco-alcohol-marijuana-use-indigenous-youth-off-reserve-schools.html

Chêne, M. (2010). *Impact of corruption on indigenous people*. https://knowledgehub.transparency.org/assets/uploads/helpdesk/245_Impact_of_corruption_on_indigenous_people.pdf

Corruption and First Nations in Canada. (n.d.). Retrieved December 15, 2022, from https://www.tandfonline.com/doi/epdf/10.1080/11926422.2016.1229685?needAccess=true&role=button

Defence, N. (2018, April 12). *Warfare In Pre-Columbian North America* [Education and awareness]. https://www.canada.ca/en/department-national-defence/services/military-history/history-heritage/popular-books/aboriginal-people-canadian-military/warfare-pre-columbian-north-america.html

Dyck, E. (2013). *Facing Eugenics: Reproduction, Sterilization, and the*

Politics of Choice. University of Toronto Press.

First Nations in Canada. (2011, June 7). [Promotional material; reference material; report; resource list]. https://www.rcaanc-cirnac.gc.ca/eng/1307460755710/1536862806124

Flanagan, T. (2017). Corruption and First Nations in Canada. *Canadian Foreign Policy Journal*, *23*(1), 15–31. https://doi.org/10.1080/11926422.2016.1229685

Forester, B. (2022, July 7). National chief alleges AFN hid $191K transfer to employee's bank account. *APTN News*. https://www.aptnnews.ca/national-news/national-chief-alleges-afn-hid-191k-transfer-to-employees-bank-account/

Hand, J. (2005). Government Corruption and Exploitation of Indigenous Peoples. *Santa Clara Journal of International Law*, *3*, 262–277.

Hanson, E. (n.d.). *Sixties Scoop*. Retrieved December 29, 2022, from https://indigenousfoundations.arts.ubc.ca/sixties_scoop/

Hopkins, A. (2014, August 1). Backlash as Canada reveals big salaries for aboriginal leaders. *Reuters*. https://www.reuters.com/article/canada-us-canada-aboriginals-idCAKBN0G14SR20140801

Indian Act | The Canadian Encyclopedia. (n.d.). Retrieved December 15, 2022, from https://www.thecanadianencyclopedia.ca/en/article/indian-act

Indigenous Peoples. (2022, June). [Text/HTML]. World Bank. https://www.worldbank.org/en/topic/indigenouspeoples

Indigenous Peoples | The Homeless Hub. (n.d.). Retrieved December 15, 2022, from https://www.homelesshub.ca/about-homelessness/

population-specific/indigenous-peoples

Indigenous peoples and communities. (2022, August 30). [Administrative page; fact sheet; resource list]. https://www.rcaanc-cirnac.gc.ca/eng/1100100013785/1529102490303

Leason, J. (2021). Forced and coerced sterilization of Indigenous women: Strengths to build upon. *Canadian Family Physician, 67*(7), 525–527. https://doi.org/10.46747/cfp.6707525

Parlee, B. L. (2015). Avoiding the Resource Curse: Indigenous Communities and Canada's Oil Sands. *World Development, 74*, 425–436. https://doi.org/10.1016/j.worlddev.2015.03.004

Porter, C., & Isai, V. (2022, January 4). Canada Pledges $31.5 Billion to Settle Fight Over Indigenous Child Welfare System. *The New York Times.* https://www.nytimes.com/2022/01/04/world/canada/canada-indigenous-children-settlement.html

Poverty and child welfare: Poverty in Indigenous and racialized communities. (n.d.). Poverty in Indigenous and Racialized Communities. Retrieved December 15, 2022, from https://oacas.libguides.com/c.php?g=702168&p=4993507

Poverty in Canada. (n.d.). Canadian Poverty Institute. Retrieved December 15, 2022, from https://www.povertyinstitute.ca/poverty-canada

Restoule, K. (2013). An Overview of the Indian Residential School System. *Ontario: Union of Ontario Indians.*

Rutherford, G. (2022, June 27). *Reproductive control of Indigenous women continues around the world, say survivors and researchers.* https://www.ualberta.ca/folio/2022/06/reproductive-control-of-indigenous-women-continues-around-the-world.html

United Nations. (2009). *State of the World's Indigenous Peoples*. United Nations.

Wilson, D., & Macdonald, D. (2010). *THE INCOME GAP BETWEEN ABORIGINAL PEOPLES AND THE REST OF CANADA*.

Zingel, A. (2019, April 18). *Indigenous women come forward with accounts of forced sterilization, says lawyer | CBC News*. CBC. https://www.cbc.ca/news/canada/north/forced-sterilization-lawsuit-could-expand-1.5102981

Social Mechanisms Facilitating Police Corruption in Canada

Aidan Lang

Culture and Corruption in Canadian Policing

A growing issue

In June 2022, the Canadian Broadcasting Corporation posted an article addressing a newly released race-based data report from the Toronto Police Service (CBC News, 2022). The data show an overwhelmingly disproportionate number of uses of force and strip searches against people of colour (Toronto Police Service, 2022). In response to this data, the Toronto Police Service developed an action plan to address issues of systemic racism within the police institution. Among the top proposed strategies are anti-Black racism and Indigenous experience training, hiring of specialized equity and inclusion instructors, and anti-bias workshops for senior officials within the service (Toronto Police Service, 2022). The CBC News article cites critics' dissatisfaction with such strategies. Notably, Dr. Notisha Massaquoi—former co-chair of the department's anti-racism advisory panel—called for individual accountability and the naming of officers involved in use of force against persons of colour, justifying her claim with: "systemic racism is created by racist people" (CBC News, 2022, para. 26).

The report conducted by the Toronto Police Service Race & Identity Based Data Team (2022) is extensive and thorough. The recognition of systemic racism on behalf of senior officials within the department is a massive step in the right direction. So too is Dr. Massasquoi's calls for individual accountability (CBC News, 2022). However, race relations training and education on marginalized experiences in Canada is not a new concept. Archived police performance reports from the Greater Toronto Area show that departments have had specific bureaus in charge of diversity and race relations since 2009 (Public Safety Canada, 2009). The disproportionate rates of use of force against marginalized groups suggest officers are operating far outside of their restraints as public servants. Further, the persistence of such conduct even when race relations have been prioritized for well over a decade suggests there is something left unaccounted for in the current analysis of police corruption on the street level.

A missing piece?

If one concept may be extrapolated from the many contributions of historian, activist, and political theorist Michel Foucault, it would be that the potential for power to operate effectively lies in its ability to remain undetected (Foucault, 1995;1975). Foucault's idea that power can operate unbridled when it is least visible is highly relevant to contemporary understandings of corruption in policing—there is a blind spot in current strategies aimed at reducing street level prejudice and discrimination.

There are many ways to define and operationalize corruption in policing. While narrower definitions of corruption may suggest instances of misconduct influenced by monetary gain, this paper defines corruption more broadly as any abuse of power or conduct causing harm that goes beyond the scope of an officer's legal duties and/or restraints (Barker & Carter, 1994). Most relevant examples today include discriminatory selection in stopping and searching of citizens and disproportionate instances of use of force against marginalized groups (Toronto Police Service, 2022). Corruption will be operationalized in this way because civilian facing interactions with the police are currently the most prioritized avenue for reform among the public and academia alike (CBC News, 2022; Campeau, 2015; Ibrahim, 2020; Wall, 2020).

Critiques and analysis of police corruption has hitherto placed much emphasis on individual police personality styles (Reiner, 2010;1984) and conservative prejudice (Gibson, 1994). However, there has been significantly less inquiry into the lesser-seen social mechanisms that may be at play in police corruption. While explorations of personality archetypes and the role of conservative ideology are crucial to understanding selection of groups to over and under police, a fulsome critique of street level corruption remains ineffective unless all factors are duly considered. Dr. Holly Campeau (2015), professor of criminology at the University of Alberta, explains how continually attacking academic issues from the same vantage point can lead to a cognitive engraving, where alternative ways of thinking about the issue become less and less accessible. Further, any new proposals for reform or training that stem from an incomplete critique run the risk of allowing the reproduction of the very issues they seek to amend.

The lack of any real improvement in civilian-facing interactions despite increased levels of racial sensitivity training among Canadian police (Government of Ontario, 2022; Public Safety Canada, 2009; Toronto Police Service, 2022) suggests that there are untapped social mechanisms at work driving hostility towards outgroups among officers. Despite higher education and training aimed at eliminating prejudicial tendencies among Canadian police officers (Government of Ontario, 2022), discriminatory practices persist, and Canadians' confidence in police has suffered as a result (Ibrahim, 2022). Several notable experiments in intergroup relations (Tajfel, 1970; Perdue et al., 1990; Maddux et al., 2008; Scheepers et al., 2009) may hold—at least in part—an explanation of prejudicial attitudes among police. Nonetheless, current theories of police personality (Reiner, 2010;1984) and conservative prejudice (Gibson, 1994) fail to address the dynamic and reactive social mechanisms officers use to negotiate meaning within their workplace (Maddux et al., 2009; Scheepers et al., 2009). In turn, police corruption continues to operate without restraint.

Prejudice and Masculinity

Scholars often seek refuge in theories of police personality when attempting to uncover the causes of corruption within departments. A common refrain is that the average police officer has maintained a relatively stable archetype throughout past decades. For many, the police officer is reliably a conservative, masculine, and cynical individual who is motivated to act first and think later (Reiner, 2010;1984). In his book "Warrior Dreams: Violence and Manhood in Post-Vietnam America," author James William Gibson paints a linear progression from a faltering sense of authoritative legitimacy—beginning with America's defeat in Vietnam—to the modern-day militarized police officer imbued with an individualistic warrior mentality (Gibson, 1994). For Gibson, America's failure in Vietnam, paired with rising rates of feminism, sparked urgent calls for the nation to re-establish its superiority through political, martial, and individual might (Gibson, 1994). Subsequently, militarization within police departments flourished both materially and ideologically (Gibson, 1994). The enemy of the warrior cop is simply a representation of the Vietnamese soldier—an enemy that Americans would have defeated had their government not imposed so many restraints. Now the warrior cop is unrestrained, and manifestations of the Vietnamese soldier are everywhere, encroaching on American land, typically from distant nations, holding unfamiliar and potentially dangerous values (Gibson, 1994).

Gibson (1994) presents an account of how existing intergroup conflicts paired with the "warrior mentality" of the modern police officer can culminate in feelings of threat and hostility when confronted with the symbolic "other." One does not have to read Gibson's work to formulate this perception of police officers. In fact, Gibson's (1994) representation of the warrior cop is exemplified in David Grossman and Loren W. Christensen's (2008) book, "On Combat: The Psychology and Physiology of Deadly Conflict in War and Peace." In their book, Grossman and Christensen (2008) coined an analogy that is now infamous for being popular among law enforcement: The analogy of the sheepdog. Grossman and Christensen (2008) categorize the whole of society into three categories. First, the sheep, who represent the societal majority. The sheep's sole purpose, according to Grossman and Christensen, is to remain productive and blissfully ignorant of the evils that exist. The evils take the form of "wolves"—the criminals of the world—those who commit harm for harm's sake. Ultimately, it is the job of the "sheepdogs"—police, military, and paramilitary figures—to confront the wolves fearlessly and allow for the sheep to remain happy and productive (Grossman & Christensen, 2008).

Predictably, calls for reform in policing, both publicly and academically, have placed much emphasis on racial sensitivity training (Toronto Police Service, 2022). However, while the warrior cop mentality is alive and well (Gibson, 1994), the causes of its manifestation may not be so easily attributed to an external threat, nor remedied by mandatory race relations training. Rather, as studies by Tajfel (1970) and Purdue et al. (1990) suggest, the manifestation of a warrior self concept is adaptively formed in an effort to maintain self esteem and simplify one's surroundings in an increasingly complex and critical environment.

Grossman and Christensen's (2008) reduction of individuals who have engaged in criminal activity to the "wolves" of the world may be seen as the most problematic aspect of the analogy. Certainly, the idea of police and military confronting "wolves" is a thinly veiled form of racist ideology, where those unlike oneself are painted as menacing and dangerous. And certainly, these problems have informed much of the literature geared towards police reform (Toronto Police Service, 2022; Reiner, 2010;1984). It may also be beneficial to highlight that the sheepdog analogy fails to account for the victim-offender overlap: a well-founded phenomenon where the individuals who engage in criminal behaviour also reliably have a long history of victimization (Berg & Schreck, 2022). This lack of recognition between what Grossman and Christensen would call "sheep" and "wolf" overlap allows for the arbitrary application of either term depending on which narrative needs to be fulfilled. Restated, sheep and wolves may not refer so much to an individual's essence, but rather, exist as a label utilized by police on an ad hoc basis to fit an acceptable narrative and justify discriminatory practices.

However, the most pervasive concept in Grossman and Christensen's (2008) analogy is that of police as "sheepdogs." The officer's need to maintain this self schema is the genesis of all outward antipathy, abuse of power, and delegitimization of civilians with which they interact. Exemplified in the Toronto Police Service's plan to prioritize equity training (2022), methods for police reform have centred on abolishing the concept of sheep and wolves—humanizing all civilians with which police have contact with. However, by tackling police corruption solely as an issue of outward prejudice, the police officer's self concept remains untouched. It is this very self concept with which systemic racism grows from. Further, calls for police reform will only serve to threaten officers' self concepts. Consequently, they will work as hard as necessary to strengthen and reaffirm themselves—a process which often relies on devaluing those outside of one's in-group (Scheepers et al., 2008).

Overrepresentation of marginalized groups in police-civilian interactions has persisted despite the existence of race relations training for well over a decade (Toronto Police Service, 2022; Public Safety Canada, 2009). Thus, dismantling the masculine and conservative police archetype is insufficient on its own for reducing street-level corruption. Moreover, attempts to reform police departments based on such attitudes have been met with strong resistance from officers (Scheepers et al., 2008; Wall, 2020). To effectively reduce discriminatory attitudes, the self concepts police officers hold must be placed under the microscope—the sheepdog (Grossman & Christensen, 2008) must be addressed.

Theories of intergroup relations

There are three well founded theories of intergroup relations that may be relevant to understanding police corruption. First, the development of groups is arbitrary (Tajfel, 1970), though this makes their consequences no less real (Jenkins, 2008). Second, discrimination toward outgroups is due to an individual's need to maintain a positive image of their ingroup—and thus, their own status—far more often than any innate outgroup antipathy (Perdue et al., 1990). Finally, when social status is threatened, stereotyping and discriminatory behaviours proliferate in an attempt to maintain legitimacy within the ingroup (Maddux et al., 2008; Scheepers et al., 2009).

Henri Tajfel was a social psychologist interested in how prejudice manifests. Individuals' self concepts—in law enforcement or otherwise—are heavily intertwined with the status of the groups they belong to (Tajfel, 1970). Individuals are adaptively motivated to preserve a positive self concept. Further, the drive to maintain a positive self concept precedes negative appraisals of out-groups. In other words, in-group and out-group appraisals are inherently arbitrary and stem from an innate attempt to cognitively simplify one's surroundings using as little processing power as possible. Adequately stated by Tajfel (1970):

> We are dealing, however, with a process that is more general and goes deeper than the learning of value judgments about a specific group and the subsequent acting out of accepted patterns of behavior toward that group. The child learns not only whom he should like or dislike in the complex social environment to which he is exposed but also something more basic. An individual constructs his own "web of social affiliations" by applying principles of order and simplification that reduce the complexity of crisscrossing human categorizations...Whenever we are confronted with a situation to which some form of intergroup categorization appears directly relevant, we are likely to act in a manner that discriminates against the outgroup and favours the ingroup. (pp. 98-99)

Tajfel understands the necessity of cognitive simplification when concerning intergroup interactions. In the case of police-civilian interactions, this process is more important than usual. For an officer to deal with every case they attend as if it were entirely new to them, or to approach any potentially dangerous individual with a curious naivety would surely translate to higher chances of not walking away from such interactions. An officer deals with hundreds of such cases per day, presumably intending to survive each one. This heightened risk exacerbates quick, automatic categorizations.

Tajfel's (1970) studies show how differential appraisals of in-groups and out-groups may be inherently arbitrary, suggesting prejudice has less to do with identifiable traits in intergroup relations but rather a need for simplification in navigating one's surroundings. Perdue et al. (1990) extends Tajfel's theory to incorporate how ingroup favouritism drives prejudice more than outgroup antipathy once such groups are formed. In their experiment, Perdue et al. (1990) conditioned participants to pair nonsense syllables ("xeh," "yof," "laj") with either ingroup (us), outgroup (them), or neutral (she) pairings. It should be noted that participants were unaware of their conditioning until a post-experiment debriefing. Participants were then asked to rate the pleasantness of each nonsense syllable. Results show that participants rated the syllable paired with their in-group as significantly more pleasant, while neutral and out-group syllables showed nonsignificant differences in rating—suggesting ingroup favouritism typically drives appraisals more than outgroup antipathy. Crucially, in their general discussion, Perdue et al (1990) make note of something that is essential to this paper's thesis:

> because in-group favoritism is often not discouraged (and may, in fact, often be encouraged; see Tajfel, 1970), the conscious, inhibiting processes that may be activated for racial bias by people who have a self-image of being nonprejudiced (Devine, 1989) may not be activated to counteract in-group–out-group bias. Thus, in-group bias may operate more openly and widely than even racial bias ("General Discussion," para. 9).

The mechanisms most commonly responsible for driving prejudice are misdiagnosed and thus allowed to operate unchecked. It should be restated that this paper does not argue against systemic racism and institutionalized discrimination. While these manifestations are very much endemic in police institutions, they may not be the essence of the problem. Restated, discriminatory practices in police-civilian interactions stem from prejudice, but prejudice itself stems from a deeper issue that continues to evade calls for reform.

Crucially, threat towards one's social status may exacerbate discriminatory behaviours and prejudicial attitudes towards outgroups (Maddux et al., 2008). In an experiment conducted by cultural social psychologist William Maddux (2008), participants were told they would be taking a test and would have their answers scored against an "opponent." If the participants scored higher, their reward for partaking in the experiment would be doubled. Participants were separated into two conditions and told their opponent would either be white or Asian.

Following the experiment, participants were rated on their affect and attitude towards Asian-Americans. Those who experienced competition and realistic threat showed significantly diminished positive attitudes and affect towards Asian-Americans (Maddux et al., 2008). Additionally, research has shown the experience of threat to have the highest effect on groups in positions of power when the status quo appears to be challenged (Scheepers et al., 2009). In an experiment conducted by Scheepers et al. (2009), researchers were interested in the reactions of dominant groups when they experienced a threat to their status. Groups were manipulated into high/low status and subjected to conditions where their status was either challenged or not. Results of the experiment show that the high-status groups displayed the most dramatic physiological responses (heightened blood pressure and pulse) when placed in a condition where their status was challenged—significantly higher than all other groups and conditions within the paradigm. Scheepers et al. (2009) discuss the implications of the results and make an especially relevant statement in support of this papers thesis:

> …the current findings remind us that in order to understand and hopefully resolve such conflicts, we should not only examine current inter-group differences or focus on existing status relations, nor should we focus on low status groups alone. Instead, we have to develop our understanding of anticipated changes in the status quo to be able to predict when and why such social identity threats arise. (p. 1090)

The critique of systemic racism in policing institutions is crucial for dismantling street-level corruption. However, without understanding the reactions of dominant groups to changing conditions, those in support of reform may encounter unforeseen resistance in areas that they are unequipped to tackle—a relevant example being the reactionary increase in solidarity among officers in the face of the Black Lives Matter movement (Wall, 2020).

Warrior for one's own sake

Evidence towards the reactionary strengthening of police solidarity can be seen in the growing popularity of "Thin Blue Line" symbolism (Wall, 2020). The Thin Blue Line logo has always stood for solidarity among police officers (Wall, 2020). Examples of such solidarity include support for officers experiencing mental illness or families of officers wounded or killed during their duties. While these concepts appear virtuous and may have originally manifested from such intentions, the use of Thin Blue Line imagery can not be separated from the contexts in which it tends to proliferate today. In the face of deafening calls for police accountability, reform, and defunding, the Thin Blue Line logo has exploded in popularity (Wall, 2020).

The reactionary use of Thin Blue Line symbolism is a clear example of how current critiques of police have manifested in perceived in-group status threat. Officers who engage in the behaviours being critiqued have "dug their heels in." Moreover, if adhering to the implications of each study conducted by Maddux et al. (2008) and Scheepers et al. (2009), current methods of police reform may motivate officers who were until now unproblematic in their conduct to adopt more prejudicial attitudes in an effort to maintain positive distinctiveness with their ingroup.

Strict adherence to race relations and victim centred approaches have ultimately led to a temporal imprinting of how critiques should be organized (Campeau, 2015). Departments have sought to address issues of conservative prejudice with race relations education (Toronto Police Service, 2022). Attempts to educate police officers on the perils of prejudice without understanding how prejudice is born has only served to strengthen officers' resistance to reform. Moreover, by repeatedly attacking issues of street-level corruption through reducing out-group antipathy, the route causes of such antipathy go unchecked and at times celebrated (Perdue et al., 1990), as displayed in the popularity of the Thin Blue Line logo (Wall, 2020).

Campeau's (2015) position complements Foucault's theories of power: The structure of the argument is just as important as the substance and, at times, may even dictate the substance itself (Foucault, 1995;1975). Training aimed at educating police officers not only on the benefits, but also, the dangers of brotherhood and solidarity is essential, lest the warrior cop (Gibson, 1994) and sheepdog (Grossman & Christensen, 2008) become reanimated and reaffirmed.

References

Barker, T., & Carter, D. L. (1994). *Police deviance* (3rd ed.). Anderson Pub. Co.

Berg, M. T., & Schreck, C. J. (2022). The meaning of the victim–offender overlap for criminological theory and crime prevention policy. *Annual Review of Criminology*, 5(1), 277–297. https://doi.org/10.1146/annurev-criminol-030920-120724

CBC News. (2022, June 15). *'We do not accept your apology,' activist tells Toronto's police chief after race-based data released.* https://www.cbc.ca/news/canada/toronto/toronto-police-race-based-data-use-force-strip-searches-1.6489151

Campeau, H. (2015) 'Police culture' at work: Making sense of police oversight, *The British Journal of Criminology*, 55(4), 669–687, https://doi-org.libaccess.lib.mcmaster.ca/10.1093/bjc/azu093

Devine, P. G. (1989). Stereotypes and prejudice: Their automatic and controlled components. *Journal of Personality and Social Psychology, 56*(1), 5-18. doi: https://doi.org/10.1037/0022-3514.56.1.5

Foucault, M. (1995) *Discipline and Punish: The birth of the prison* (2nd ed.) Vintage Books. (Original work published 1975).

Gibson, J. W. (1994). *Warrior dreams: Violence and manhood in post-Vietnam America.* Hill and Wang, a division of Farrar, Straus and Giroux.

Grossman, D. & Christensen, L. W. (2008). *On combat: The psychology and physiology of deadly conflict in war and peace.* Warrior Science Pub.

Government of Ontario. (2022, June 22). *OPS inclusion & diversity blueprint.* Ontario.ca. https://www.ontario.ca/page/ops-inclusion-diversity-blueprint

Ibrahim, D. (2020, November 25). *Public perceptions of the police in Canada's provinces, 2019.* Statistics Canada. https://www150.statcan.gc.ca/n1/pub/85-002-x/2020001/article/00014-eng.htm

Jenkins, R. (2008). Nations and Nationalisms. In *Rethinking Ethnicity* (2nd ed). SAGE Publications Ltd. https://doi.org/10.4135/9781446214855.n10

Maddux, W. W., Galinsky, A. D., Cuddy, A. J. C., & Polifroni, M. (2008). When Being a Model Minority Is Good . . . and Bad: Realistic Threat Explains Negativity Toward Asian Americans. *Personality & Social Psychology Bulletin, 34*(1), 74–89. https://doi.org/10.1177/0146167207309195

Public Safety Canada. (2009, November 26). *Peel regional police annual performance report* [Archived PDF]. Government of Canada. https://www.publicsafety.gc.ca/lbrr/archives/cnmcs-plcng/cn31779-2009-eng.pdf

Perdue, C. W., Dovidio, J. F., Gurtman, M. B., & Tyler, R. B. (1990). Us and Them: Social Categorization and the Process of Intergroup Bias. *Journal of Personality and Social Psychology, 59*(3), 475–486. https://doi.org/10.1037/0022-3514.59.3.475

Reiner, R. (2010). *The politics of the police*. Oxford University Press. (Original work published 1984).

Scheepers, D., Ellemers, N., & Sintemaartensdijk, N. (2009). Suffering from the possibility of status loss: Physiological responses to social identity threat in high status groups. European Journal of Social Psychology, 39(6), 1075–1092. https://doi.org/10.1002/ejsp.609

Tajfel, H. (1970). Experiments in intergroup discrimination. *Scientific American, 223*(5), 96-103. https://doi.org/10.1038/scientificamerican1170-96

Toronto Police Service Race & Identity Based Data Team. (2022). Race & identity-based data collection strategy: Understanding use of force & strip searches in 2020 [Detailed Report]. Toronto Police Service Public Safety Data Portal. https://data.torontopolice.on.ca/pages/race-based-data

Wall, T. (2020). The police invention of humanity: Notes on the "thin blue line." Crime, Media, Culture, 16(3), 319–336. https://doi.org/10.1177/1741659019873757

Corruption and Education

Khushi Shah

The Oxford English Dictionary defines corruption as *dishonest or illegal behaviour, especially of people in authority*. Education is arguably one of the most important aspects of life as with such a lot of doors are opened for individuals, which are not offered to those without. Generation after generation the power and importance of education is only further highlighted, thus more and more children are pursuing higher education. As such, the number of students enrolled in schooling worldwide has been on an upwards trajectory, with an increase of over 150 million students since 2000 for secondary school and around 82 million since 2000 for primary school (Statista, 2022). Furthermore, the completion rate of primary school was close to 90% in 2019 and 76% for secondary school (Statista, 2022). Education can provide individuals with so many options and aid in their life path by increasing the aspects of stability in life, financial stability, equality between individuals worldwide, self-dependence, confidence, provides safety, and helps one reach their goals (Nair, 2022). In Canada itself, more than 1.4 million students are enrolled in a Canadian University, and 2.2 million students are enrolled in some form of postsecondary education (Universities Canada, 2018).

Even though the importance of education is highlighted and with such, the statistics of students pursuing education is increasing every year, there are still a lot of children who are being refused education, do not have access to it, cannot afford further studies, and more. Worldwide 16% of girls were not enrolled in secondary school whereas 15% of boys were not in 2018 (Statista, 2022). Africa has the most children not in school, being 39% of girls and 36% of boys not in school there (Statista, 2022). Females in particular are also denied the right to education pursuits such as secondary school and postsecondary learning due to the ongoing cycles of exploitation and discrimination, these patterns being more present in poorer countries. Save the Children, Educate Girls, Give, TheirWorld, CARE, United World Schools, We, and more to name a few are all charity-based non-profit institutions that work hard to provide children with the resources, finances, and living conditions to be given their right to education.

Corruption present in educational institutions only adds to this decline, forcing more students to be unable to access education and stripping them of their basic rights. Corruption in education fosters in many different ways leading to detrimental effects on the students. These aspects include the regulatory systems, teaching roles, admissions, recruitments, assessments, test taking, credentials and qualifications, research roles, and through research publications (Glendinning et al., 2019). Although corruption in education runs worldwide, some countries such as Russia, Nigeria, India, and the 11 countries part of the Western Balkans are more aware of such corruption compared to more developed countries such as North American and Scandinavian countries (Glendinning et al., 2019).

Corruption usually lies within the regulatory bodies and leadership teams of education institutions, but on the contrary, 64% of respondents from those categories expressed that they did not believe there is any corruption in their regulatory processes (Glendinning et al., 2019). The leadership with confidence believes that their respective organizations have means and methods to ensure there is no corruption in the regulatory processes. A global study conducted for the Council for Higher Education Accreditation International Quality Group concluded after examination of various institutions that to minimize corruption in their regulatory systems it is important to practice transparency: including how officials are appointed and the systems report publications, leadership must follow an integrity code, only select officials who have integrity and no history of conflicts, reducing bureaucracy, have one authority figure responsible for receiving all complaints and appeals, and to start having more random visits to check the quality, as well as how well the rules against corruption are being upheld (Glendinning et al., 2019).

Furthermore, higher education systems also have a lot of corruption in the form of political interference including overriding research funding decisions, putting a ban on subjects from the curriculum, and even imprisoning those in the education system who do not abide by the rules and beliefs of the prevailing politics (Glendinning et al., 2019). Some countries that had the highest prevalence of such include Australia, Brazil, Hungary, Poland, Russia, Turkey, India, and the USA (Glendinning et al., 2019). With teaching positions becoming more scarce, academics feel hopeless and begin to accept bribes as means to secure a job. For example in India, 1200 colleges are affiliated with the same university, and with the rotation of teachers, not many jobs are available (Glendinning et al., 2019). In Russia, a prominent issue of postsecondary institution leaders and professors having fake or unqualified doctorate degree is also leading to corruption (Glendinning et al., 2019). Injustices are more likely to occur as the institution representatives themselves do not respect ethical practices, and they lack the academic qualification and accreditation where they monitor others' responsibility to set the academic standard. Not only this but when higher education institutions are made aware of the fake degree or thesis, the committee members responsible for verifying and awarding such doctoral degrees should also be held accountable (Glendinning et al., 2019). For example, a committee consisting of the same advisors who approve doctoral dissertations in Russia were linked to support more than 50 other plagiarized or fake dissertations, in Russia (Glendinning et al., 2019). Problems with charging and acknowledging these forms of corruption as an abuse of authority is difficult as institutions do not want to shed light on the fact, nor do they want to use any finances for such. Additionally, a lot of in-breeding occurs within educational places, where they favour their own graduates and students rather than having a fair system for students within their population and from outside. In-breeding in institutions is a major issue in Western Balkan countries and Russia (Glendinning et al., 2019).

Another aspect where corruption may play a part is that the standards set for higher education systems are not consistent worldwide. This system does not allow for the same quality, preparedness, and ability of differing professionals worldwide. For example, in India even after obtaining a university degree, there are various tests needed to be taken to be able to perform jobs, whereas this is not the same in all other countries (Glendinning et al., 2019). Another example included medical school, as in North America you have to finish university to apply, but in other countries, you can apply straight after high school; and the length of medical curriculum and requirements also differ greatly throughout (Glendinning et al., 2019). Moreover, gender discrimination leads to corruption as well and is still present to this day. An example of such is that in a few Japanese universities there is a system that officials have placed that do not allow for more than 30% of the medical graduates to be females (Glendinning et al., 2019). In Africa, a survey was conducted where over 1200 participants commented on gender-based corruption and the results were that 42.6% stated it was present in higher education institutions, and 57.3% stated it was present in private education institutions (Mbonyinshuti, 2022).

Corruption within the teaching role itself accounts for a lot as well, and the issues can be due to trying to massify education systems, increase the school's reputation, increase ranking, financial pressures, and more. Due to teachers' salaries not being very high, even though the amount of work deserves a much higher salary and the fact that not many teaching positions are open this leads to a lot of job insecurity. Forcing academics to have multiple short-term or more casual teaching options the susceptibility of accepting bribes increases to change students' grades or overall report cards as well (Glendinning et al., 2019). There is also the aspect of absenteeism by academics which entails of leaving teaching and supervision tasks to teaching assistants, research students, and junior colleges, which is highly unfair and is taking advantage. This phenomenon termed *ghost advising* is very prominent in Kosovo due to a shortage of qualified academics with the right credentials (Glendinning et al., 2019). Corruption also occurs through teachers by harassment, whether that be bullying, verbal, sexual, or otherwise. For example, teachers will be found to demand sexual favours from students if they want their grades to be changed, which leads to a lot of sexual harassment issues. Students are also known to physically abuse their teachers due to various reasons in Uganda (Glendinning et al., 2019).

In order to further explore corruption in education, looking at the admissions process and requirements in higher education institutions is one of the main areas corruption exists. In a global study conducted in 2018, the highest concern in this area was regarding the advertising and recruitment process being misleading of higher education institutions (Glendinning et al., 2019). After such, the following concerns were regarding falsified transcripts, falsified or nonauthentic recommendation letters, and cheating in admissions tests (Glendinning et al., 2019). Favouritism misleading and making decision-making unfair for students have been highly reported in both Japan and Slovakia (Glendinning et al., 2019). A series of highly organized and systematic corruption in education was investigated and reported on by journalists working from Canada, USA, Australia, and the UK. These corrupt practices include faking qualifications in order to get a visa to get admission abroad, having student admissions based on bribery, using one political connections for admission, nepotism, allowing sports stars admission without them having the relative academic requirements, and cheating by having someone else take English language tests needed for acceptance (Glendinning et al., 2019). Corruption in the admissions process is a major issue as when students are accepted using the various forms of corruption discussed above they are in reality underqualified for the program (Glendinning et al., 2019). This means that they do not have the language skills, academic experience, or knowledge in order to succeed. These students tend to suffer a lot after their admission leading to their mental health plummeting, feeling vulnerable, feeling depressed, and may even resort to cheating to just get by (Glendinning et al., 2019).

Based on the global questionnaire completed, the most common forms of corruption within student assessments were plagiarism and cheating in assessments, cheating in examinations, and having paid another person to do the work; thus, the work is not authentically by the student which deems them unworthy of the mark as well (Glendinning et al., 2019). These forms of corruption can play out by when teachers allow it to happen by accepting student bribes and favours. Additionally, leaking test information and helping students discreetly during examinations by academics in higher institutions also occurred. Students themselves add to this corruption by having a third party take the examination for them, having them complete an assignment, stealing notes from peers, and going to the various, and building in popularity essay writers who do the work for them for a fee. With the growth of students plagiarising and cheating institutions have also increased their use of credibility-checking systems. For example, in the majority of Canadian universities and secondary schools as well any work turned in online is automatically checked by Turnitin. Slovakia, Slovenia, and the UK have started to purchase plagiarism detection software as well to decrease corruption and increase both the credibility and reliability of student assessments (Glendinning et al., 2019). Moreover, Australia and the UK are creating strict guidelines, New Zealand and Ireland are adding new legislation that states companies that promote and advertise cheating are illegal, New Zeland and the USA are prosecuting more corruption in student assessments by taking it more seriously, and lastly, worldwide there is more research being conducted regarding how to address academic corruption and to increase academic integrity (Glendinning et al., 2019). South-East Europe has found that when corruption through bribery have higher consequences established through institutions such as police involvement, it is effective in decreasing such (Glendinning et al., 2019). Based on the global questionnaire it was reported that participants believe institutions need to be strict and have serious consequences in regards to examination security, detecting plagiarism, handling plagiarism, enforcing fairness, and ensuring fraud does not take place.

Another major corruption sector in universities and higher academic institutions is regarding graduation, qualifications, and credentials. Based on the global questionnaire this category was one of the highest on what corruption mainly entails in education (Glendinning et al., 2019). Types of corruption in this area include degree mills, accreditation mills, falsified degrees, fake transcripts, and false information put on resumes, plus applications (Glendinning et al., 2019). A degree or accreditation mill is when a company or an organization is claiming to be an academically credited educational institution, but in reality produces fake degrees, qualifications, and diplomas. These places are very harmful as they lead to the decrease in credibility of real academic places and lower the quality, plus the importance of such degrees, qualifications, and diplomas given out by actual credited educational institutions. One of the ways that the degree and accreditation mill issue is being solved is with the GDN, the Groningen Declaration Network (Glendinning et al., 2019). In the GDN, they have an international network of credited academic organizations and educational institutions from which they are able to support various reviewing processes by verifying whether academic qualifications are falsified or real (Glendinning et al., 2019). Furthermore, this issue of having fake qualifications becomes extremely pressing when these individuals who do not deserve it, are hired and become active practitioners of responsible jobs such as in healthcare and engineering. Potentially, corruption in this sense can also lead to the loss of life of multiple innocent individuals, due to one corrupt one. Society understands that this is a major issue ad as such many researchers, journalists, and others have investigated individuals in high positions' accreditations (Glendinning et al., 2019). The results led to a lot of falsified degrees being identified with the consequence of their master's and doctoral degrees being revoked (Glendinning et al., 2019). More examples include Germany revocating Ph.D. awards to unqualified medics, discovering the scam of the Pakistan diploma mill which a lot of individuals from the USA, Canada, and the UK for caught, Russia taking back degrees that were wrongfully obtained, and over 8'000 plagiarised dissertations found thus far (Glendinning et al., 2019).

The lowest form of corruption in higher education institutions is through research and academic publications. Although, for many universities, their research and publications are one of the main contributors regarding how they are ranked globally for their qualifications and academic standing. In this section of corruption, it is expressed through academic publication plagiarism, supervisors crediting their student's work as their own, the peer review process being unethical, and the inability to present results that were inconvenient (Glendinning et al., 2019). The peer review process is very important in research and education as by such plagiarism is caught, studies are held up to the highest professional levels, and only accurate data conclusions made through credible studies are then published for the world to review (Glendinning et al., 2019). The peer review process becomes unethical where bribery is used and where peer reviews actively suppress the research done by their rivals. One of the biggest scandals regarding corruption within research and academic publishing occurred in the US

NIH (National Institute of Health), where rules and restrictions had to be made to Duke University in 2015 (Glendinning et al., 2019). These sanctions and restrictions were necessary as financial irregularities and irresponsible supervision of many of their research projects, one of them being cancer research led to malpractice incidents. In China, Sweden, and the UK, even the national government has been made aware of these corruption issues in which they are starting to strengthen the codes of ethics in research in order to address the delinquency in academic research and publications (Glendinning et al., 2019). The USA also has their own office called the ORI, the Office of Research Integrity which is responsible for investigating misconduct and unethical research (Glendinning et al., 2019). Research can be retracted due to a variety of causes such as research being conducted in a non-standardized manner, framing the research data to meet what the research wants the results to show, the inability of other research papers to duplicate such fabricated results, plagiarism, and lastly, falsification. In order to reduce the stigma of humiliation and career-ending through retractions, when a genuine mistake has been made authors are encouraged to retract and fix their mistake. This way other papers and research conducted on the basis of such papers will not be affected. The research publication industry also has many journals that are like the previously mentioned degree and accreditation mills as they are not real journals with a real peer review process (Glendinning et al., 2019). Publishing in this kind of journal or any disreputable journal is highly discouraged as through such the corruption in research and publishing increases.

Throughout the chapter methods of how corruption in higher education systems can be countered, addressed, and fixed have been discussed. Moreover, networking with the Accreditation and Quality Assurance Body, also known as AQAB is one of the best ways to get help in managing such corruption (Glendinning et al., 2019). The AQAB's often times collaborate with other educational organizations and academic institutions on a local, national, and global level which means that they have ties to higher powers and are able to spread the word easily (Glendinning et al., 2019). Journalists are also a great networking tool to fight corruption in higher education systems as they spread awareness of such and also are known to aid the AQAB's in the investigative process to find issues, plus find strategies to counteract them (Glendinning et al., 2019). Organizations such as the Committee of Publication Ethics, also known as COPE, PubPeer, and Retraction Watch all are working hard with their volunteers in order to combat corruption (Glendinning et al., 2019). Thus, it is important that institutions, journalists, and the AQAB's all work together in order to raise awareness about concerns and the immense amount of corruption that occurs in education, research, and publication. Based on the global questionnaire completed regarding corruption in various higher education institutions the following 11 conclusions were made in recommendation for accreditation and quality assurare practices: to review terms regarding corruption in the organization, report and make further changes to the terms in order to better address corruption when malpractice is taking place, explicitly make it a point to talk about corruption to combat it, allow for transparency in order to uphold accountability and integrity in the institution, to be vigilant about corrupt indivudals and not be afriad to go against them in order to keep a higher standard, being pro-active and responsible by responding to any corruption, have the AQAB's come for an inspection at short notice, providing the AQAB's support in developing standards and rules for educational and researhc quality, use higher education leadership to promote integrity, network internationally not only locally to find ways to fight corruption as many place sin the world are going through similar situations, be a leader to advocate against diploma mills and accreditation mills, and lastly, conduct more research on corruption within higher education systems in order to inform others, better the policies, and better adress exaclty what forms of courruption, misconduct, and unethical behavours are occurring in these institutions (Glendinning et al., 2019).

Thus, corruption is a huge problem in the higher education and research systems, and it is imperative that these areas be addressed and further researched so that solutions can be found. The categories discussed include the regulatory systems, teaching roles, admissions, recruitments, assessments, test taking, credentials and qualifications, research roles, research publications, and methods to combat such corruption.

References

Education worldwide - statistics & facts. Statista. (2022, October 11). https://www.statista.com/ topics/7785/education-worldwide/#topicOverview

Facts and stats. Universities Canada. (2018, July 31). https://www.univcan.ca/universities/ facts-and-stats/

Glendinning, I., Stella-Maris, O., & King, A. (2019, February). *Policies and actions of accreditation and quality assurance bodies to corruption in higher education.* Unesco. https://etico.iiep.unesco.org/en/policies-and-actions-accreditation-and-quality-assurance-bodies-counter-corruption-higher-education

Mbonyinshuti, J. A. (2022, October 12). *Gender-based corruption widespread in universities – report.* University World News. https://www.universityworldnews.com/post.php?story=20221012075549801#:~:text=According%20to%20the%20report%2C%20the,level%20was%20indicated%20as%2057.3%25

Nair, M. (2022, November 22). *Why is education important: All the reasons to stay in school.* University of the People. https://www.uopeople.edu/blog/10-reasons-why-is-education-important/

Corruption's Impact on Economic Development

Madhumita Nathani

What is Corruption?

Corruption is behaviour lacking integrity by individuals in positions of power, whether they operate individually or as part of a larger organization (Chen, 2022). Examples include governments offering greater resources to wealthy individuals or households, public officers accepting bribes in exchange for actions, and politicians misusing public money (Chen, 2022). Often, corruption is able to occur due to additional professionals who support the main individual in power – lawyers, accountants, and other agents (*What is corruption?*).

What is Economic Development?

Economic development in the long term is defined by two factors: growth in the labour force, and growth in the productivity of the labour force (Chad Stone et al., 2017). Growth in the labour force can be influenced by a change in a country's demographics like the age of the population, immigration policies, economic policies like taxes, and sociocultural beliefs and norms. Productivity growth is influenced by investments in capital, an increase in the education, motivation, and skill level of the labour force, and overall innovation in the country (Chad Stone et al., 2017). The political and institutional environment also affects each of these factors. Corruption erodes public trust and consumer confidence, weakens democracy, hinders economic development, and further exacerbates any pre-existing inequality and other divides in the country (*What is corruption?*).

Types of Corruption

Corruption can be defined by certain categories: supply and demand corruption, conventional and unconventional corruption, grand and petty corruption, and public and private corruption (*Definitions of Corruption* 2022). Supply-side or active corruption refers to offering a payment or advantage, whereas demand-side or passive corruption involves the acceptance of a payment or advantage (*Definitions of Corruption* 2022). Conventional corruption is when a payment or advantage is received but there is an expectation of reciprocity – supply and demand corruption fall under this category (*Definitions of Corruption* 2022). Unconventional corruption, on the other hand, is when an individual acts without integrity with the goal of personal gain. In this case, since there is no actual transaction, there is no expectation of reciprocity. Examples of unconventional corruption include embezzlement and theft. Grand and petty corruption also fall under conventional corruption, with grand corruption involving incentives offered regarding larger-scale government projects like construction (*Definitions of Corruption* 2022). Public corruption and private corruption are distinguished by the sectors committing the illicit act, with public corruption involving a public official on one side of the act, and private corruption involving only those in the private sector.

General Impact of Corruption on Economic Development

Firm Productivity

One main aspect of economic growth is growth in an individual firm's productivity. World Bank Data on Indian firms finds that corruption negatively impacts company resource allocation, subsequently halting new product innovation and development (*The impact of corruption - Knowledge Hub*). Corruption also makes the labour force less efficient (output per employee per hour) – a 2006 study focusing on corruption's impact on labour efficiency across 13 Latin American countries found that countries in which corruption was more prevalent needed a larger labour force to achieve the same amount of output as countries in which corruption was less prevalent (*The impact of corruption - Knowledge Hub*). In a similar vein, corruption diverts human resources and talent away from productive tasks towards seemingly more lucrative actions (*The impact of corruption - Knowledge Hub*).

Foreign Investment

Foreign direct investment (FDI) also impacts economic growth. It supports the creation of new jobs, improvements in infrastructure, and investments in human capital, ultimately leading to higher production and incomes. When launching operations and seeking investment opportunities in new countries, investors typically look for political stability and institutional support (Karadima, 2022). Countries that have higher amounts of corruption typically lack in stability, making these countries less likely to gain FDI and experience lower economic growth as a result. Corruption also works like a tax on FDI coming into a country, making the investments less effective than they can be because of the misallocation of money.

Income Inequality

Another aspect of economic development is income inequality within the country. One major aspect of income inequality is uneven wealth distribution between the poor and rich, which corruption exacerbates through growth, asset, tax system, and social program channels (Gupta, 1998). A country that experiences high growth rates also experiences higher rates of poverty reduction; since corruption reduces the overall growth of a nation, it subsequently slows improvements in a country's poverty problem (Gupta, 1998). In countries with high levels of corruption, a small segment of the population owns large amounts of assets. These owners use their wealth as leverage to gain better exchange rates and tax treatment on their assets, increasing their earnings and reducing returns earned by the poorer population (Gupta, 1998). As such, corruption increases income inequality through the asset ownership channel. The tax channel is similar, with tax systems being more biased in countries with high levels of corruption, disproportionately affecting poorer groups of people and increasing income inequality as a result (Gupta, 1998). With bribery being tolerated in countries with corruption, the operating costs of governments and other social groups increases, reducing government spending on things like education and health that directly benefit disadvantaged groups in society (Gupta, 1998). Going back to growth, increases in income inequality through the aforementioned channels reduce growth and further limit improvement in poverty issues.

Another aspect of income inequality is gender inequality. Research by Transparency International in 2014 revealed that there is a positive relationship between corruption and female mortality rates; with the number of mothers dying during childbirth increasing exponentially in countries where bribery is a norm, gender inequality is increased (*Link between corruption and gender inequality*). Additionally, around 70% of the population below the poverty line are women, meaning the misallocation of public resources and services directly hinders women from leaving poverty, further deepening the gender divide in corrupt countries (*Link between corruption and gender inequality*).

Consumer Confidence
Finally, widespread corruption can reduce the confidence of consumers and businesses. Though not impacted directly, consumer sentiment about the economy in a country greatly influences consumer spending

that constitutes 65% of total GDP (*Consumer confidence* 2022). Two metrics that quantify consumer confidence are the Consumer Confidence Index (CCI) and the Consumer Sentiment Index. If consumers believe their country is corrupt, they may be less likely to spend on purchases or make investments, decreasing capital investment that spurs economic growth (*Consumer confidence* 2022).

Case Study: South Africa

African countries experience prolonged poverty, unequal distribution of wealth, and slow economic growth. Among developing countries, South Africa has made the slowest progress in improving its living standards (Gyimah-Brempong, 2001). Alongside poor economic development, African countries experience rampant corruption, with two African countries being identified as the most corrupt countries globally (Gyimah-Brempong, 2001).

The Corruption Perceptions Index (CPI) ranked South Africa with a score of 44 out of 100 in 2015, with 100 being the least corrupt and any score under 50 signalling high corruption (*KPMG International* 2017). The score has been on a decreasing trend from 56 in 1995 to 50 in 2000 to 44 in 2015, indicating South Africa is becoming more corrupt over time (*KPMG International* 2017). With private investment contributing directly to output, there is a strong negative correlation between corruption and output due to corruption decreasing levels of investment.

Petty corruption is rampant in South Africa's public sector, with bribes usually being paid to traffic officers, police officers, and employment officials. This costs companies from 2.5-4.5% of their sales, translating to a 20% decrease in labour costs (*Corruption in South Africa* 2020). Tax revenue decreases as a result and the wealthy often evade paying taxes through bribes (*Corruption in South Africa* 2020), perpetuating a biased tax system where the 'poor get poorer', negatively affecting income inequality which is a main factor for quality of life and economic development.

Corruption affects South African socioeconomic status in other ways as well. Resources like transfer payments and foreign financial aid are diverted through bribery and ulterior motives (*Corruption in South Africa* 2020). The usage of public funds and resources places downward pressure on companies, resulting in job loss and an increase in the unemployment rate. Unemployment in South Africa is extremely high, with only 6.2 million of 19.7 million youth (ages 15-35) being employed (*Corruption in South Africa* 2020). This reduces output and GDP as a result. Employment is at risk mainly for low-income earners who constitute a relatively large proportion of South Africa's population (*Corruption in South Africa* 2020). Corruption directly affects individuals in this class, further increasing the wealth inequality. 49.2% of South Africa's adult population lives before the poverty line (*Corruption in South Africa* 2020).

Nepotism and state capture, where a few people are in control of the government's resources, also negatively impact South Africa's economy. Nepotism causes unfair treatment and biased decision-making, causing important economic sectors to be staffed with less skilled individuals who have connections to people in power (*Corruption in South Africa* 2020). This also hinders competition and innovation in the long term, influencing another factor for labour productivity. Sociocultural views play a role in how nepotism is tolerated in South Africa, allowing it to happen. Research conducted by The Conversation finds that 73% of respondents support public officers favouring individuals they know over more competent applicants (*Corruption in South Africa*2020).

Corruption was further exacerbated during the pandemic from the misallocation of COVID-19 relief funds. Originally meant to procure personal protective equipment (PPE) like masks, gloves, and face shields, help low-income households with food parcels, and support local small businesses, health workers still suffered from lacking protective gear and having low salaries (Africa News, 2020). This was due to the funds being overpriced with potential fraud able to pass undetected due to few people monitoring transactions (Africa News, 2020).

Case Study: South Korea

South Korea's economy is dominated by chaebols, its conglomerates, who have a large economic and political influence. There are 40 chaebols in South Korea, with the largest few comprising majority of Korea's economic output – the traded shares of the biggest four, Samsung, LG, Hyundai, and SK, compose half of the domestic stock market (*The Chaebol of South Korea* 2022). Chaebols closely work with the government and government support through loans and tax incentives contribute to their success (*South Korea's Chaebol Challenge*). Candidates for the election aim to have the chaebols on their side due to the scale of their influence.

Many top executives from chaebols including Samsung, Hyundai, Lotte, and SK have been found guilty of corruption. These executives can afford to pay heavy fines or receive presidential pardons due to their close relationship with the government, setting them free even if convicted (*South Korea's Chaebol Challenge*). Due to chaebol control over the country's resources, judges often also make biased decisions in court that benefit founding families of chaebols (Park et al., 2021). Media companies are also influenced in these situations, publishing pieces in support of the chaebol executives in fear of the power of chaebols.

In contrast to corruption's impact on South Africa's economy, corruption has not been solely detrimental to South Korea's economy. The rise of chaebols began with the 1960 President Park Chung-Hee, who agreed with capitalist firm owners that the government would provide their firms monopolistic privileges and cheap borrowing from banks as long as the firms meet mandated export targets (*South Korea: Corruption that built its economy*). This incentivized investment, innovation, output, and economic growth as a whole. The growth enhancing corruption-growth model has now been spreading to countries in Southeast Asia, including Indonesia, Thailand, and Malaysia.

While chaebols can be credited for most of South Korea's investments in research and development (R&D), they can also harm the economy by reducing competition. These conglomerates are so large that they are often monopolistic, having the power to use their brand name to copy innovations from and squeeze small and medium enterprises (SMES) out of the economy (Park et al., 2021). This decline in competition greatly affects economic growth, with South Korea's export growth slowing from a rate of 12% annually over the years 2001-2011 to a rate of 3% from the years 2011-2017 (Park et al., 2021). Once these chaebols have their exclusive supply chains developed, they are also able to pressure and decrease prices of supplies since suppliers know they will not obtain the same scale of business with any alternative buyers (Park et al., 2021). Since supplier profits have now declined, they have less incentive to innovate, harming long-run factors of economic growth like labour productivity.

Case Study: United States of America

Before the COVID-19 pandemic played its role in the U.S. economy, Donald Trump's tax policies favoured the upper-class population. Trump's Tax Cuts and Jobs Act in December 2017 provided tax breaks to corporations and wealthier individuals with a decrease in the corporate income tax rate from 35% to 21% (*ABC News*). This was in turn financed by government borrowing that took away from money that could have financed the government's response to the COVID-19 pandemic, in turn increasing national debt (*ABC News*). Exacerbated by Trump's downplaying of the pandemic's severity, less government spending on social programs for individuals who had lost their jobs during the pandemic increased income inequality, especially for Black and Hispanic groups that formed the majority of non-essential, destroyed positions (*ABC News*).

Donald Trump also repealed the Fair Pay and Safe Workplaces Executive Order, which enforces compliance from federal contractors on worker protection laws (Hananel Director et al., 2022). By doing so, millions of workers in the United States are left vulnerable to discrimination, forced arbitration, and wage theft, since the government will not have eyes on prior labour law violations before assigning contracts (Hananel Director et al., 2022). This increases corruption in the United States and directly increases income inequality and decreases worker morale.

Trump has also taken actions that work against the Affordable Care Act (ACA), which mainly comprises health insurance reforms and tax provisions affecting the U.S. population. Trump supported efforts to repeal the ACA that involved repealing the 3.8% net investment income tax (Hananel Director et al., 2022). This tax directly funds ACA programs that maintain quality of life standards and retirement security for the working population. While this action directly harms the working population, this selfish choice would have saved Trump $3.2 million dollars in taxes in a single year, exacerbating the wealth divide (Hananel Director et al., 2022). Trump had further cause to support repealing the ACA; doing so would reduce his taxes by over $2 million while stripping health insurance away from 24 million Americans (Hananel Director et al., 2022).

While engaging in activities that benefit him financially, Trump also reneged on his earlier promise to disclose his tax returns, leaving the rest of the population unaware about whether proposed reforms would benefit Trump or the working population (Hananel Director et al., 2022). This raises distrust and suspicion of corruption amongst the working population, further diminishing consumer confidence and labour productivity through the motivation channel. Additionally, he proposed budget cuts for many programs that support small business development and entrepreneurs, decreasing competition in the market and strengthening existing monopolies (Hananel Director et al., 2022).

Combating Corruption

There are some measures in place to help prevent corruption at the country level through changes to systems and implementing incentives. The World Bank's Anticorruption Initiatives aim to address the corruption problem with a focus on developing countries alongside integrating behavioural psychology in its actions (World Bank Group, 2022). The COVID-19 pandemic has led to large amounts of government emergency spending which, in the absence of proper protocols, can be used in other ways. This was explored in the South African case study above, reducing the effectiveness of such emergency measures. The lack of transparency and incentives to stay honest opened the doors to corruption, and these must be enforced for governments to remain accountable (World Bank Group, 2022).

Certain countries are taking steps to prevent corruption. Afghanistan has made its procurement system transparent through making information on procurement process available on the public National Procurement Authority (NPA) website. The increased amount of oversight has helped the government save $270 million (World Bank Group, 2022). In Brazil, the World Bank helped develop an artificial intelligence system that identifies potential fraud in public procurement processes, high-risk cases, corrupt firms, and public servants who may be engaging in dishonest behaviour (World Bank Group, 2022). In Kenya, the World Bank is helping create a data analytics system that can monitor performance of the judicial system to identify corruption risks (World Bank Group, 2022). In Ukraine, the World Bank has helped create an asset declaration system (World Bank Group, 2022). In Serbia, the Bank is helping create a platform for all stakeholders to convene on progressive actions to address corruption, and in Mongolia, the Bank is ensuring expenditure information can be accessed online (World Bank Group, 2022). These measures help direct government funds where they are most useful for economic development, increasing growth, decreasing inequality, and increasing labour productivity.

The World Bank Group plays a crucial role in forming international transparency standards like the Asset Disclosure Standards, supports international anti-corruption alliances and forums like the G20 Anti-Corruption Working Group, and assists countries with identifying sources of illicit flows of money and stolen assets (World Bank Group, 2022).

Conclusion

Corruption is a major obstacle to economic development. When corrupt governments and officials abuse their positions of power and influence, it creates an uneven playing field for businesses and working individuals. It discourages investment and innovation, as foreign investors and entrepreneurs may be unwilling to risk their capital in a system that is not transparent or fair. Corruption also diverts resources away from where they are needed most; instead of being used to fund public services or infrastructure projects that benefit the broader community, they go to wealthy individuals. This can have serious consequences, as it can lead to a lack of improvement in education, healthcare, and transportation, which are all essential for economic development and equality. Combating corruption is therefore crucial for promoting economic growth and improving the standard of living for all members of society.

References

ABC News Network. (n.d.). ABC News. Retrieved December 30, 2022, from https://abcnews.go.com/Business/trumps-economic-legacy/story?id=74760051

Admin, P. by D. D. P. (2020, October 6). *Implication of corruption on economic growth in South Africa.* DDP Blog. Retrieved December 16, 2022, from https://ddp.org.za/blog/2020/10/06/implication-of-corruption-on-economic-growth-in-south-africa/

AfricaNews. (2020, September 3). *South Africans protest as report reveals Covid-Relief Fund misuse.* Africanews. Retrieved December 16, 2022, from https://www.africanews.com/2020/09/03/south-africans-protest-as-report-reveals-covid-relief-fund-misuse/

By Chad Stone, More from the Authors Chad Stone Areas of Expertise, Chad Stone Areas of Expertise Federal Budget Economy Climate Change Immigration Recent Work: , Recent Work: Senate Revenue Package Is Sound Policy 3 Reasons Why Inflation Fears Shouldn't Block a Well-Designed Economic Package Inflation Misperceptions Cloud Policy Debate, & Senate Revenue Package Is Sound Policy 3 Reasons Why Inflation Fears Shouldn't Block a Well-Designed Economic Package Inflation Misperceptions Cloud Policy Debate. (2017, April 27). *Economic growth: Causes, benefits, and current limits.* Center on Budget and Policy Priorities. Retrieved December 16, 2022, from https://www.cbpp.org/research/economy/economic-growth-causes-benefits-and-current-limits

Canada, P. S. (2022, August 3). *Definitions of corruption - research brief no. 48*. Public Safety Canada. Retrieved December 16, 2022, from https://www.publicsafety.gc.ca/cnt/rsrcs/pblctns/rgnzd-crm-brf-48/

The chaebol of South Korea: The conglomerates that dominate the Korean economy. Foreign Brief. (2022, August 6). Retrieved December 16, 2022, from https://www.foreignbrief.com/analysis/the-rulers-of-south-korea/

Chen, J. (2022, October 13). *Corruption: Its meaning, type, and real-world example*. Investopedia. Retrieved December 16, 2022, from https://www.investopedia.com/terms/c/corruption.asp

Council on Foreign Relations. (n.d.). *South Korea's Chaebol Challenge*. Council on Foreign Relations. Retrieved December 16, 2022, from https://www.cfr.org/backgrounder/south-koreas-chaebol-challenge

Gupta, M. S. (1998, May 1). *Does corruption affect income inequality and poverty?* imfsg. Retrieved December 30, 2022, from https://www.elibrary.imf.org/view/journals/001/1998/076/article-A001-en.xml

Gyimah-Brempong, K. (2001). *Corruption, economic growth, and income inequality in Africa*. College of Arts and Sciences | University of South Florida. Retrieved December 16, 2022, from https://www.usf.edu/arts-sciences/

Hananel Director, S., Hananel, S., Director, Director, M. C. A., Coleman, M., Director, A., Manager, S. N. S. M., Nadeau, S., Manager, S. M., President, J. C. V., Cusick, J., President, V., Gordon Director, P., Gordon, P., Director, J. P. S., Parshall, J., Director, S., Associate, G. G. P. and O., Griffin, G., ... Ives-Rublee, M. (2022, August 23). *100 ways, in 100 days, that Trump has hurt Americans*. Center for American Progress. Retrieved December 30, 2022, from https://www.americanprogress.org/

article/100-ways-100-days-trump-hurt-americans/

Karadima, S. (2022, April 19). *Is corruption a barrier to FDI? it's complicated...* Investment Monitor. Retrieved December 30, 2022, from https://www.investmentmonitor.ai/features/fdi-corruption-investment-transparency/

The link between corruption and gender inequality: A heavy burden for development and democracy. Wilson Center. (n.d.). Retrieved December 30, 2022, from https://www.wilsoncenter.org/publication/the-link-between-corruption-and-gender-inequality-heavy-burden-for-development-and

The impact of corruption on growth and inequality - knowledge hub. (n.d.). Retrieved December 16, 2022, from https://knowledgehub.transparency.org/assets/uploads/helpdesk/Impact_of_corruption_on_growth_and_inequality_2014.pdf

KPMG International. KPMG. (n.d.). Retrieved December 16, 2022, from https://home.kpmg/za/en/home.html

Park, S., Schwak, J., Kim, H.-A., Triggs, A., Watson, I., Dawkins, A., Editors, E. A. F., Lee, Y.-jung, Bruns, S., Hlasny, V., Arao, D. A., Tsuya, N., Park, J., Lee-Makiyama, H., Cook, A. D. B., & *, N. (2021, March 24). *Chaebol reforms are crucial for South Korea's future.* East Asia Forum. Retrieved December 16, 2022, from https://www.eastasiaforum.org/2021/03/24/chaebol-reforms-are-crucial-for-south-koreas-future/

South Korea: The corruption that built its economy. IIAS. (n.d.). Retrieved December 16, 2022, from https://www.iias.asia/the-newsletter/article/south-korea-corruption-built-its-economy

Team, T. I. (2022, July 13). *Consumer confidence: A killer statistic.* Investopedia. Retrieved December 30, 2022, from https://www.investopedia.com/articles/fundamental/103002.asp

What is corruption? Transparency.org. (n.d.). Retrieved December 16, 2022, from https://www.transparency.org/en/what-is-corruption

World Bank Group. (2022, May 19). *Combating corruption.* World Bank. Retrieved December 30, 2022, from https://www.worldbank.org/en/topic/governance/brief/anti-corruption

The Effects of Corruption on National Security

Bareeha Shamsi

Introduction

When acts of corruption undermine the law of a country, the nation begins to experience a downfall. Citizens of a nation place their trust in higher powers that they believe will guide their nation to prosperity and wealth. However, these individuals abuse their power for personal monetary gain. People of a nation don't choose the route to corruption out of nowhere, although if they experience financial problems or are stuck in a tight space, they consider taking routes which benefit nobody but themselves. A nation remains solid and congruent by strengthening its internal and external affairs, which all fall within the realm of National Security. National security is a pillar upon which a nation relies intensely. An extremely crucial aspect that determines a nation's stability and protection, along with the comfort of those residing within. National security acts as countries stabilizer. It impacts the country's foreign relations and how a country may seem in the eyes of the world. A crack in national security will impact the country's structure and push the nation down a vicious circle. The rule of law, economic development, and security are all concepts parallel to national security. Once corruption enters the boundaries of a nation, national security is the first to take the hit, which indicates the downfall of all these pillars as well.

Weakening the Rule of Law

Corruption once emphasized, becomes a way of life many individuals choose to follow. The ones fascinated by this ideology run after great power and destroy anything coming their way. When more extraordinary powers within a country's government come under the bounds of corruption, the individuals residing within those borders become affected by them. Individuals with power manipulate the legal system to work according to their actions. In this process, they pay massive bribes while committing theft and illegal tax evasion (Council of Europe, 2021). Bribes, tax evasion, and theft can be seen as the most prominent global signs of corruption and an indication of a failed legal system. Many civilians are preyed upon due to these acts and are forced to suffer for necessities. Corruption has many dangerous aspects; bribery is the biggest one pushing everything else into its corrupt standpoints (Knowledge, 2013). In a corrupt economy, bribery is the most significant motive which leads to the deterioration of a legal system. When individuals can buy their way through, they no longer respect the restrictions and boundaries that were once set in place. A Nation such as Mexico once had a strong and stable constitution. However, once corruption reached the judicial system, the judicial system was broken, and so was the country's defense against foreigners (Dlewis, 2022). Mexico has slowly become a country where individuals can no longer be held accountable for their actions. Due to the massive overload of corruption, anyone with power can mold the system in whichever way they desire. The legal system has been undermined to such an extent that individuals no longer look up to it. Only 1.3% of criminal cases are solved; the rest are either closed off with the help of bribes or are never reported due to the lack of faith civilians have (Dlewis, 2022). Over one year, European developing countries experienced a $1.6 trillion US loss due to extreme participation in bribes, tax evasion, and theft (Council of Europe, 2021). Due to the immense amounts of illegal activities, individuals refrained from paying the government the proper dues. Instead, they put that money in places that would benefit them. This causes the government to be short on money and, therefore, require more to give back to the economy. Pakistan, a country of great resources and technology, is now a land of corruption where individuals act as if there is no legal system. Due to the extent of corruption, the citizens could not fight against it, so they decided to become one with it. More than half of the individuals living in Pakistan have bribed law enforcement personnel for their gain (World Justice Project, 2017). On the other hand, a quarter of the population has bribed the police to process their desired government permits (World Justice Project, 2017). Once an institution is no longer congruent and authoritative, individuals begin to undermine its power and use it to their advantage. The government of Pakistan is wholly disfigured due to corruption. Across the globe, one can see many more countries suffering from similar issues. Countries around Europe, Asia and even South America all suffer from extreme cases of corruption. Columbia is one of the highest corruption indexes ranked countries and has fully lost the trust of their civilians. 61% of Columbian citizens believe that the police and military are corrupt therefor are unwilling to abide by the country's laws and regulations (Philipp, 2020). The constant bribery that takes place in the legal system has removed all respect for law and order and is slowly beginning to lose its meaning completely. As the people noticed the corrupt behaviors of government officials, the crime rates began to rise. The country faces a 39.7% annual increase in crime rates which cannot be helped nor contained unless corruption is put to an end (Philipp, 2020). These countries struggle with a weakened legal system due to the corruption that has polluted their land. The influential individuals who stood on the country's most trustworthy and authoritative stand, had used the country's assets for personal gain. This forced the citizens to look after themselves, and a corrupt country does not allow high-morale workers to live freely. The Columbian judicial system has reached a place in which a large percentage of the judges are unqualified (Colombia country risk report 2020). The only reason why they were able to achieve a position in such a high platform, was all due to the bribes they had paid. These paid bribes have allowed unqualified individuals to sit in court and make decisions regarding a nation, and its people. Because of improper judicial systems, three-quarters of Columbian businesses face corruption and loss (Colombia country risk report 2020). Once a nation's laws begin to deteriorate, individuals set themselves in a 'flight or fight' mode. This leaves struggling individuals to work through corruption, and as the government gets its way, the citizens shall also get theirs.

Economic Development and Global Affairs

An economy's well-being is a highly crucial aspect of national security. When a nation struggles to protect its borders, many foreign entities can intercede and operate the country's vital aspects according to its likability. In many situations, countries worldwide step in and take advantage of specific resources because they are aware that certain economies cannot allocate those resources properly (Mirzayev, 2022). Corruption can lead to inefficiencies in the use of resources and the delivery of public goods and services, which can have a negative impact on productivity and economic growth. This can also create an uneven playing field in which specific individuals or groups can gain an unfair advantage, leading to a lack of competitiveness and innovation (Mirzayev, 2022). In an economy, companies can select their suppliers through a process called the tender process, in which they can receive the best quality resources at the best prices (Kenton, 2022). Although this is a concept that all businesses have access to, not all businesses are qualified for this resource. In a corrupt economy, many companies bribe their way into the system and receive the best resources, and misuse it to their advantage. They put back into the economy the remainder of their resources (Mirzayev, 2022). Despite all the benefits these corrupt individuals receive, they are still eager to gain more profit which causes them to participate in tax evasion.

Due to tax evasion being such a huge aspect of corrupted economies, Columbia has also had its fair share of it. On a yearly basis, six to eight percent of the nation's GDP is lost due to tax evasion (Partz, 2022). Despite tax evasion being such a serious federal crime, individuals tend to take it very easily. This connects back to how the system is very weak and has caused individuals to rid themselves of the fear that comes with the judicial system. Corruption varies from different acts around various aspects of a nation, businesses tend to be major targets for corruption. Individuals are able to benefit themselves and put others at a loss by putting the names of their businesses upfront. The tender process seems to be a very common procedure done by many businesses.

Corruption acts within the tender process can be seen around many continents around the world, Including South Asian country's such as Pakistan. Many Pakistani construction companies such as IESCO can get contracts without having to go through proper tendering processes. Along with that, they are able to get contracts and construction done without the requirement of legal documentation (Ahmadani, 2022). These individuals are able to use the name of their powerful companies and begin processes which would take certain companies to fulfill in a span of years. They are able to do this by corrupting the legal processes and altering them to their personal desires (Ahmadani, 2022). Many countries around the world that are corrupt are able to alter many aspects of businesses, governments as well as laws and regulations of a country.

A weakened government results in external operations which happen without congruent policies and contracts which give both parties security. When corruption takes place, many fo the contracts and policies are undermined which causes harm to one if not more of the parties involved. Many nations under the effects of corruption cannot interact in the global economy due to their sinful ways. For a country to prosper in the global economy, it must refrain from corruption and participate in international relationships. Although when corruption takes part in a federation's operations, the desired outcome is rarely attained. Misallocation of fund or resources results in process being unattainable or delayed. The nation of Columbia comes face to face with losses due to corruption on a daily, they annually lose a certain percentage of GDP specifically to corruption. Consistent economical downfalls influence individuals to view businesses as unreliable and inefficient, it also causes international countries to view Columbia as a high-risk business partner as the nation suffers from a trade deficit (Philipp, 2020). Losing a certain GDP percentage indicates that the money which could be placed into improving both international and domestic businesses is now being stored elsewhere leaving behind an unsteady economy.

Encountering a loss in both domestic and international businesses impact the nation greatly. Not only are the people involved in the businesses effected but so is the entire economy. A country with little to no international trade becomes incompetent in the eyes of the world and is unable to uphold their international status (Knowledge, 2013). As a nation, being able to participate in foreign trade and businesses happens to be a great aspect of success, although corrupt countries are unable to do such due to their broken systems.

Effectiveness of Security Forces

Once a nation is taken over by a fraudulent entity, the weakening of its assets has already begun. Not only does corruption destroy legal systems and economies, but it makes this a possibility by enabling its ability to weaken a country's border. Buying into a country's military or intelligence agencies is not difficult if the rest of the country is quickly sold for monetary profit. Countries such as Mexico and Columbia are full of corruption; because of that, their borders have weakened, allowing anyone to come through (Knowledge, 2013). When a country struggles economically, it is easier for foreign bodies to intervene. One can see that around the world, countries that face significant corruption also face major smuggling and human-trafficking operations (Council of Europe, 2021). One can look towards Columbia, a country with tremendous resources, although due to its inability to allocate them correctly the nation has faced a tremendous loss of business relations and wealth (Philipp, 2020).

Columbia is one of the world's most beautiful pieces of land. However, because the leaders of this nation have practiced corruption for several years now, the country operates upon bribes and illegal affairs, which make the land susceptible to foreign threats. This is a nation that is extremely rich in resources yet, due to its embezzlement they are of no use. Due to the government's inability to use the resources correctly, it was as if the nation never had resources, to begin with. The country is significantly impacted by smuggling and trafficking (Goff, 2022). Corruption on a land spread as if it were a plague. Once it enters the government, it enables many illegal activities, which include open access to a country's border. Foreign entities having access to the borders of a nation allows them access to control and use the country's resources, assets, and forces to their advantage (Philipp, 2020). Smuggling and trafficking are two immediate effects of corruption. Throughout the years, Columbian children are being child trafficked on a daily. While the number of child trafficking exceeds a thousand, only 50 cases were provided justice (2021 trafficking in person report - United states department of state 2021). Suppose a corrupt official accepts bribes in exchange for awarding contracts or grants to specific companies or individuals. The allocated resources may not go to the most deserving or qualified recipients. This restricts the state from implementing proper security infrastructures or proper responses to external and internal threats. If the right resources were put towards strengthening the borders and legal systems, people would not suffer in such ways. The main reason to why Columbian trafficking statistics had been going sky-high connected back to the corruption within the policing sectors. The police were aware of many criminal activities regarding sex trafficking as well as child trafficking. Although as the police came close to a raid, many officers who had been bribed by these criminal organizations would inform the human traffickers (*United States Department of State,* 2022).

The citizens of Columbia have begun to lose their trust in their government due their inability to provide necessary security and regulations. Where many Columbian citizens were being faithful and paid the government the right amount of taxes and being faithful. The same government receiving that money was putting it to incorrect use. The people of the nation lost their money, as well as lost the trust a country should instill within its people. Corruption is extremely common to the point where forty-eight thousand government officials have been accused of corruption and have gone through investigations (Philipp, 2020). The lack of faith the citizens have in their system is valid, not only are the policing sectors corrupt but so are the military and national defenses. The country's largest drug smugglers and rebel groups have gained authority over the country's highest level of military personnel. They were able to bribe the officials in return for information which will keep them out of prison (Bronstein, 2007). The head of one of the largest cartels in Columbia was also able to bribe army officers and plan a break-out for his brother out of one of the country's high-security prisons (Bronstein, 2007). This demonstrates how criminals can bribe their way into the system, protect themselves and if any obstacles come in their way, once again they are able to bribe their way through.

Through such events, one could examine how corruption in national security leads to an extensive impact on how the walls of the country protect what lies within and stand firm against what tries to intercede. A nation can remain extremely sturdy and competent when it comes to military and government officials. Although, when corruption takes place, these officers are not being paid well and therefore are forced to take corruptions hand to feed their families.

Conclusion

Corruption itself is a disease, one that darkens every light it comes across. Countries that come across corruption remain stuck with it until someone comes forward willing to take a huge revolutionary stand. National Security is the most congruent aspect of a nation, it consists of the country's economy, security, law, and order, as well as international relations. Corruption does not spark out of thin air; it is ignited with greed and selfishness. Individuals begin using their surroundings for personal gain and slowly expand onto putting everything in their domain. One may use the same monetary gain to have access to more authority, this is achievable through corruption's biggest asset; bribery. All corrupt countries located around the world expanding from Asia to South Africa, have reached their own individual peaks of corruption. Yet they all started off with the first step of bribery. This step expands onto the final downfall of a nation's national security. An anti-corruption nation is not unattainable, although it is difficult to achieve. The use of bribery has allowed corrupt individuals to take part in many illegal activities without them having to face severe consequences. These activities include tax evasion, smuggling, human trafficking, resource embezzlement as well as judicial bylaws. When countries take the initiative to go over their system thoroughly and examine where they fall weak, they can see much improvement. Many nations have taken initiative to create new policies which hold authoritative figures accountable for their actions. Where many judges, military, and police personnel can roam their way through freely, now they will be held accountable. To strengthen a country's national security, the individuals running the government should be those who are qualified and reliable. When governments fail to proceed with moral actions, not only does the nation experience a huge downfall, but so do the individuals living within its border. Corruption is an immoral act that causes governments and countries to lose sight of the big picture, which is the betterment of the nation and its people. When people begin putting their personal gains before the countries, it harms the individuals

References

Ahmadani, A. (2022, November 27). Corruption, misuse of authority by IESCO officials goes unchecked. PT. Retrieved December 30, 2022, from https://www.pakistantoday.com.pk/2022/11/28/corruption-misuse-of-author.ty-by-iesco-officials-goes-unchecked/

Bronstein, H. (2007, July 30). Colombia admits high-level military corruption. Reuters. Retrieved December 30, 2022, form https://www.reuters.com/article/us-colombia-corruption-army-idUSN3042454420070730

Colombia country risk report. GAN Integrity. (2020, November 4). Retrieved December 30, 2022, from https://ganintegrity.com/countty-profiles/colombia/

Partz, H. (2022, August 17). Colombia to prevent tax evasion with National Digital Currency: Report. Cointelegraph. Retrieved December 30, 2022, from https://cointelegraph.com/news/colombia-to-prevent-tax-evasion-with-national-digital-currency-report

Philipp, J. (2020, January 18). 10 facts about corruption in Colombia. The Borgen Project. Retrieved December 30, 2022, from https://borgenproject.org/10-facts-about-corruption-in-colombia/

U.S Department of State. (2022, July 19). 2022 trafficking in persons report - united states department of state. 2022 Trafficking in Persons

Report: Colombia. Retrieved December 30, 2022, from https://www.state.gov/reports/2022-trafficking-in-persons-report/

Council of Europe. (2021, July 7). Corruption undermines human rights and the rule of law - commissioner for human rights - publi.coe.int. Commissioner for Human Rights. Retrieved December 16, 2022, from https://www.coe.int/en/web/commissioner/-/corruption-undermines-human-rights-and-the-rule-of-law

Dlewis. (2022, June 3). Failing justice in Mexico: The multi-layered problem of Crime. Vision of Humanity. Retrieved December 16, 2022, from https://www.visionofhumanity.org/failing-justice-mexicos-institutional-weaknesses/

Goff, P. (2022, November 16). Human trafficking in Colombia. The Exodus Road. Retrieved December 16, 2022, from https://theexodusroad.com/human-trafficking-in-colombia/

Kenton, W. (2022, September 26). Tender in finance definition: How it works, with example. Investopedia. Retrieved December 16, 2022, from https://www.investopedia.com/terms/t/tender.asp

Knowledge, H. B. S. W. (2013, November 5). The real cost of bribery. Forbes. Retrieved December 16, 2022, from https://www.forbes.com/sites/hbsworkingknowledge/2013/11/05/the-real-cost-of-bribery/?sh=8d7cd1173e8b

Mirzayev, E. (2022, July 18). The economic and social effects of corruption. Investopedia. Retrieved December 16, 2022, from https://www.investopedia.com/articles/investing/012215/how-corruption-affects-emerging-economies.asp

U.S. Department of State. (2021, September 14). 2021 trafficking in persons report - united states department of state. U.S. Department of State. Retrieved December 16, 2022, from https://www.state.gov/reports/2021-trafficking-in-persons-report/

World Bank Group. (2022, May 19). Combating corruption. World Bank. Retrieved December 16, 2022, from https://www.worldbank.org/en/topic/governance/brief/anti-corruption

World Justice Project Pakistan Justice Sector Survey 2016. (2017). The rule of law in Pakistan. World Justice Project. Retrieved December 16, 2022, from https://worldjusticeproject.org/our-work/wjp-rule-law-index/special-reports/rule-law-pakistan

Corruption in the Workplace

Marcile Wilmot

Introduction

Corruption is a word that is all too familiar in our world today, and in recent years it has garnered a lot more attention, due in part to the increasing awareness of its negative impacts through the efforts of many anti-corruption initiatives. Though complex and multifaceted, it is certainly not a new phenomenon in society, "[with] the earliest records... dat[ing] back to the thirteenth century BC, to the time of the Assyrian civilization" (Sumah, 2018). Yet, "Until the 1980s, corruption was mainly a topic of political, sociological, historical, and criminal law research and just recently came to the fore in the fields of economics. [Now], with the increasing quality and availability of data, empirical research on corruption has taken off since the late 1990s, whose insights [are imperative in] generat[ing] better targeted and more effective anti-corruption policy measures. (Lambsdorff and Schulze, 2015, as cited in Dimant and Tosato, 2017). Fast-forward to today, and these measures are still largely theoretical. Corruption is still a global and long-standing issue, and one that cannot be easily done away with. And it is present not only in underdeveloped countries but in public and private corporations as well. As a result, it can manifest in many different arenas and in various ways. This chapter will focus on corruption in the workplace (in both the public and private sectors but primarily the private sector), what that looks like and the negative impacts its presence can have on businesses and the market at large. The truth is that although many businesses suffer as a result of corruption, many also have an active role in perpetuating the problem. Obvious obstacles stand in the way of finding the solution to such issues, as it is neither an instantaneous nor straightforward process. Thus, we will also discuss methods for identifying corruption and offering strategies for preventing and or mitigating these practices in the workforce. That being said, it is imperative that the reader has a clear understanding of what corruption is.

Understanding Corruption

We will now examine several different definitions of the word to get a clearer picture of its meaning. According to research done by Sumah, "the word corruption is derived from the Latin word "corruptus," which means "corrupted" and, in legal terms, the abuse of a trusted position in one of the branches of power (executive, legislative, and judicial) or in political or other organizations with the intention of obtaining material benefit which is not legally justified for itself or for others (Sumah, 2018). The Merriam-webster dictionary definition of corruption is, "dishonest or illegal behavior especially by powerful people (such as government officials or police officers)" (Merriam-Webster, n.d.). And finally, the definition given by transparency international (TI) is that it is "the abuse of entrusted power for private gain" (Transparency International, 2022). Corruption then broadly defines any action taken by a powerful person, or organization with the intent of profiting at the expense of another. It is a serious offense that takes many forms such as embezzlement, bribery, kickbacks, conflicts of interests, and abuse of power to name a few. And it is not just a growing problem in the public and private sectors in Canada, but it is present in many other countries as well. In fact, according to the corruption perception index (CPI) "…the most widely- used global corruption ranking in the world…corruption levels are at a worldwide standstill…with no significant progress [being made] against corruption in the last decade (Transparency International, 2022). The reality that little seems to be effective in the fight against corruption is a cause for great concern, as the effects are undeniable and far-reaching. "Corruption undermines the rule of law, impacts negatively on the business environment and national budgets, and affects citizens' everyday life in areas such as healthcare and education. The pervasiveness of corruption enables infiltration of organized crime groups into the public and private sector" (UNODC Statistics and Surveys section, 2013). The question then becomes, why? Why are the efforts put forth by various organizations to prevent corruption proving futile? The answer, if there is one, lies in understanding the reasons why corruption exists in the first place. Any attempts to discover them is an important first step in beginning to address the issue.

Causes of Corruption in the workforce

There are several causes that contribute to the issue of corruption in the workforce and perhaps many of them will remain unknown. However, five in particular will be discussed in this section, the first of which is competition.

Competition:
Though it is believed and argued by many that competition is one of the ways to decrease the prevalence of corruption in the workforce, many studies have found reason to believe otherwise. [One] "...study that looked at market competition using firm-level data to try to overcome difficulties from looking at cross-country data found that stronger product market competition is associated with an increase in the levels of corruption" (Alexeev and Song, 2013 as cited in Dimant and Tosato, 2017). "Where they have occurred, liberalization and deregulation have fostered a market driven by intense competition, leading companies to engage in corruption to maximize operational efficiency, safeguard

development, and conquer new markets (Pakstaitis 2019, as cited in Kiener-Manu n.d.). Similarly, according to research done by Carmen Nobel, "…many organizations in highly competitive markets are likely to bend the rules if doing so will keep their customers from leaving for a rival firm (Nobel, 2012). To expand upon this, let us take a moment to define liberalization and deregulation, two terms that are commonly used together. Firstly, "Liberalization is the process of relaxation from government control… it means the reductions in applied restrictions of the government on international trade and capital. Deregulation is the disappearance of state restrictions on both domestic and international business" (tutorialspoint, 2022). Generally, this is thought to have many benefits such as opening up investment and employment opportunities, decreasing monopolies especially in the public sector, and encouraging different goods and services at fair prices. "However, the process of economic liberalization—including privatization, deregulation, etc.—often appears associated with an increase, often a dramatic increase, in corruption" (Stephenson, 2014).

Economic Downturn:

Another driver for corruption within businesses is economic downturn, because "unfortunately, corruption can appear to be a workable and effective business practice for survival and growth. If maximizing profit by any means is seen as the sole company objective, then evaluating the potential costs versus benefits of corruption can seem like a legitimate exercise- which may justify corruption" (UNODC Statistics and Surveys section, 2013). In fact, "according to the World Bank survey in 2019, 20% of companies across 139 countries were asked for at least one bribe" (Strategic direction, 2021). As staying in business and remaining profitable is essential to the success of any company, it is not difficult to see how engaging in a few unethical practices seems a viable and even necessary option to some. Businesspeople on occasion also justify corruption as a win-win situation where no one gets hurt (Alliance for Integrity, 2016 as cited in UNODC Statistics and Surveys section,

2013). In fact, Alesia Nahirny, executive director of TI Canada, the leading anti-corruption NGO in the country, says that until just over a decade ago, paying bribes to win business or speed up transactions was widely seen as "a necessary evil" (Trade commissioner service, 2016). Thus, the issue arises where these practices are not viewed as unethical in the first place, and "rationalization strategies" emerge as a way of justifying them. According to behavioral science, some people will cheat to gain an advantage if they are able to rationalize their behavior and still feel good about themselves (Ariely, 2013 as cited in UNODC, 2013). In regard to private sector corruption, UNODC lists three types of rationalizations observed which we will look at below.

1) "Everyone is else is doing it:"

When unethical behavior is normalized across a group within a company or in the entire company (or industry), there is no sanction for engaging in the behavior... When individuals perceive that their competitors are engaging in corrupt practices, they can justify undertaking comparable actions with the rationale of securing the company's well-being as well as their personal well-being, while still feeling that they are a "good" person (Johannsen and others, 2016 as cited in UNODC, 2013). Thus, rationalization is also referred to as a "collective action problem" (Persson, Rothstein, and Teorell, 2013 as cited in UNODC, 2013).

2) "It's not my responsibility:"

Individuals rationalize engagement in corruption as being beyond their control. Typically cited reasons for employees trying to deny responsibility are: "I didn't know that was corruption"; "I didn't do it for me; I did it for my organization"; "I don't know how to respond to corruption" (Alliance for Integrity, 2016 as cited in UNODC, 2013).

3) "The end justifies the means:"

"Corruption can be perceived as generating positive collective effects, because it- however incorrectly- appears to be in the company's best interests. [It] can also be rationalized because it has positive effects for individuals, such as enabling them to keep their jobs" (UNODC Statistics and Surveys section, 2013).

Another important consideration is that "culturally... corruption may have become a habitual way of doing business within some companies and in some countries" (Strategic direction, 2021). Economic and individual causes of corruption can lead to the development of (and be supported by) a corporate culture of corruption. And this "culture of corruption... becomes both an outcome and a further cause of corruption" (UNODC, 2013). Thus, this will be the next point of discussion.

A Corporate Culture of Corruption:
According to Xiaoding Liu, "corporate corruption culture is... defined as the shared values and beliefs of a firm's employees [and is] calculated as the average corruption attitudes of insiders (i.e., officers and directors) of a company (2016). Some scholars who are especially attentive to cultural variations consider Western anti-corruption norms to be ethnocentric and even a source of cultural imperialism. Their key claim is that payments, gifts, and favors play a legitimate role in the social fabric of many cultures, even when they are assailed in Western societies as corrupt (UNODC, 2013, p.22). Still, there is no one specific cause as, "a corporate culture of corruption is brought about by a multiplicity of factors such as competition and growth orientation, complicated leadership structures, and high levels of autonomy and discretion, with a lack of transparency, accountability, and ethics" (UNODC, 2013). A few factors Taylor (2016) suggests can contribute to and normalize this culture. These are, "when corruption is embedded

in the structure and processes of a company, the perpetuation of self-serving ideologies that justify corrupt practices and new employees being socialized into tolerating and permitting corruption" (2016). Other factors include, when growth in a company is the primary goal, when competition is high, when the leadership is complacent, and when there is low transparency in the company. This brings us to the next point and possible driver for corruption in the workforce, which is a lack of transparency.

Lack of Transparency:

"Theory suggests that increased transparency should be associated with lower levels of corruption [because] with increased transparency, the probability of detecting wrongdoing increases, as does the accountability of each decision maker" (Dimant and Tosato, 2017). What then is transparency? According to UNODC (2013) it is, "a situation in which information about a decision-making process is made publicly available and can easily be verified both in terms of the rules and the identities of the decision makers [which] increases the probability of the detection of corruption". The issue that arises, primarily in the private sector, is that "it is characterized by freedom of action, initiative, mutual agreements, informal reconciliation of interests and decision- making, spontaneity, lower accountability and control, and the fact that business cannot forego gifts. And although the private sector requires transparency and morality, it cannot be expected that the same level of transparency will be ensured as in the public sector" (Pakstaitis, 2019). Research done by Tom Collins presents that, "the difficulty in making any real headway is the innate opaqueness of the private sector... [because] these powerful companies exert huge economic and political influence, yet we continue to know too little about them" (2019). With the problem of corruption, similar approaches are being taken to fight against it in both the public and private sectors. This, however, is proving ineffective as, "it remains unclear in what manner crimes committed by businesses should be pursued as corruption, because business practices such as gifts and agreements, discounts, favors for partner are customary in the business sphere, something that is not allowed in the public sector" (Pakstaitis, 2019). Consequently, this is considered one of the main drivers for corruption in the business place.

The Impact of Corruption on Businesses

We've taken time to discuss some of the possible causes behind corruption in the workforce and now it is imperative that we discuss the impacts of it. An accurate estimation of the effects of corruption on businesses is difficult to arrive at, due to a deficiency in research regarding this. However, from what little information there is, important conclusions can still be drawn. "Private corruption affects the entire supply chain, as it distorts markets, undermines competition, and increases costs to firms. It prevents a fair and efficient private sector, reduces the quality of products and services, and leads to missed business opportunities (UNODC, 2013).

"The organization for Economic co-operation and development estimates that the cost of corruption equals more than 5 percent of global GDP (US$ 2.6 trillion), with some US$1 trillion paid in bribes each year. The World Economic Forum reports that corruption increases the cost of doing business by up to 10 percent, on average. Transparency International (TI) says that corruption in government procurement processes can add as much as 50 percent to a project's costs" (Trade commissioner service, 2016). That being so, perhaps the most significant impact that corruption has on businesses is economic in nature which we will explore below in addition to two other major impacts of corruption. The information below is taken from research from the United Nations Office on Drugs and Crime.

Economic cost of corruption

Although obtaining exact figures on the economic costs of corruption is difficult, a 2016 report from the International Monetary Fund 12 (IMF) estimated the cost of bribery alone to be between $1.5 to $2 trillion per year. This represents a total economic loss of approximately 2% of global GDP (UNODC, 2013, p.13).

Poverty and Inequality

According to the World Bank (2019 as cited in UNODC, 2013), more than 50% of the population of the oil-rich country live in extreme poverty. This example shows that as political and economic systems are enlisted in the service of corrupt actors, wealth is redistributed to the least needy sources. Mechanisms such as political representation and economic efficiency are both compromised by self-dealing and secret exchanges. Under conditions of corruption, funding for education, health care, poverty relief, and elections and political parties' operating expenses can become a source of personal enrichment for party officials, bureaucrats, and contractors. Social programmes and the redistributive potential of political systems suffer accordingly. A key result of all the instances named above is a state of unequal opportunity in which advantages arise only for those within a corrupt network (UNODC, 2013, p.14).

Dysfunction in public and private sector

The cumulative effect of individual corrupt acts is dysfunctionality. Whether offered by the public or private sectors, the quality of goods and services decrease, and the process of obtaining them becomes more expensive, time consuming and unfair… [The result is that] corporations lose the incentive to offer better services and products if they can undermine competitors through obtaining political favors (UNODC, 2013, p.14).

These are only a few of the many impacts that corruption has on businesses, but the main take-away is that it is an enormously destructive force. The question then becomes, is it really possible to fight against this? And if so, how? This will be discussed in the next section.

Fighting Against Corruption

In the fight against corruption in businesses and other sectors, it would appear that having stricter rules and regulations would be a step in the right direction. Yet, UNODC (2013) believes that "focusing on rules and regulations alone will often fall short of meeting [the] higher expectations of ethical business practices. [Thus, as a tactic against corruption they recommend an] "…ethics and compliance programme that… aims to foster a culture of integrity. This is considered beneficial for the companies as, "engaging in efforts to prevent corruption makes good business sense given the negative impact corruption can have on individual businesses and the market as a whole (UNODC, 2013). Secondly, this culture of integrity is one that must be communicated and demonstrated from top-level management consistently. After all, employees will observe and duplicate what they see being done by their leaders. "To overcome a corporate culture of wrongdoing, top management needs to make clear that it does not advocate or condone wrongdoing, and that after a proper root cause analysis and investigation, intentional corruption will be punished. In technical jargon, this is often referred to as "tone from the top ''. Such a policy of zero-tolerance of corruption should be communicated within a framework that couples the stick of punishment with the carrot of a positive message about the type of behavior that the company expects from its employees" (UNODC, 2013). Finally, as a means for combating corruption "behavioral change approaches based on value-based programmes" seem to be widely effective in encouraging awareness and change in the area of ethics among employees. Value-based programmes are premised on the assumption that employees engage with whichever values are present in the company, pro-social or anti-social, and adopt them as their own. When these values are oriented towards pro-social engagement, employees are more likely to comply with rules, even when they are not monitored. Key elements in value-based programmes are treating employees fairly, rewarding ethical behavior, remedying unintentional unethical behavior, and punishing criminal behavior (Treviño and others, 2006 as cited in UNODC, 2013).

Conclusion

In this article, we looked at corruption, the history of it, its meaning, some possible causes for it, and ways that it can be prevented in businesses/ the workplace. Though the issue of corruption is a very present and ongoing one especially in the public sector, it may not look the same in the private sector and may not respond to the same measures. Thus, beyond stricter rules and regulations, several studies discovered that developing ways to increase the level of ethical awareness among companies and their employees may be the most effective method in fighting corruption in the long-term. Therefore, this should certainly be an area of focus for anti-corruption organizations in future research.

References

Corruption. (2022). In Merriam-Webster.com dictionary. Retrieved December 7, 2020, from https://www.merriam-webster.com/dictionary/corruption

Dimant, E., & Tosato, G. (2017). In Journal of Economic Surveys (2018) Vol. 32, No.2, pp. 335-356. "Causes and effects of Corruption: What has past decade's empirical research taught us?" John Wiley & Sons Ltd. https://content.ebscohost.com/cds/retrieve?content=AQICAHioQh6va-Q1f_660avHqehX5LEStxh3GpqBCg7yJ_AGctQFs1taabR9D4ff7tk2cO-

4bLAAAA4zCB4AYJKoZIhvcNAQcGoIHSMIHPAgEAMIHJBgkqhki-
G9w0BBwEwHgYJYIZIAWUDBAEuMBEEDM2k-l5XlWGMuEHG_
AIBEICBm-6p1XMBhP0Y4TQ-NW-uU0XopIEHE0eFYHGGYNAM-
TOWqjjVf2iYzft4gTprFgqWmSfOA-o4o0Dne7AB2ANP-0TeX4P2o-
bhDP1OFb4Xi-rhr2au1SSwCabykQ9PBLcrB6x-sE1t3kgyOW3556vpH-
jdLNZDfy0mG6dU6yuOcsQOpYURcEVateIrWh4MlF-k057P9rb9p-
KAQ6v_v6QK

Kiener-Manu, Katharina. (n.d.). "Cause of Private Sector Corruption". United Nations Office on Drugs and Crime. https://www.unodc.org/e4j/zh/anti-corruption/module-5/key-issues/causes-of-private-sector-corruption.html#:~:text=A%20corporate%20culture%20of%20corruption%20is%20brought%20about%20by%20a,of%20transparency%2C%20accountability%20and%20ethics

Liu, Xiaoding, (2016). "Corruption Culture and Corporate Misconduct". Harvard Law School Forum on Corporate Governance. https://corpgov.law.harvard.edu/2016/11/29/corruption-culture-and-corporate-misconduct/

Nobel, Carmen. (2012, December 30). "Competition Leads to Workplace Corruption, Research Shows." HBS Working Knowledge. Pakstaitis, Laurynas. (2019, January 26). "Private sector corruption: realities, difficulties of comprehension, causes and perspectives. The Lithuanian approach". Crime, law, and social change (2019) 72:227-247. Springer Nature B.V. 2019. https://content.ebscohost.com/cds/retrieve?content=AQICAHioQh6vaQ1f_660avHqehX5LEStxh3G-pqBCg7yJ_AGctQENSTs9YNm4fDp5BOcyQTYHAAAA4zCB4AY-JKoZIhvcNAQcGoIHSMIHPAgEAMIHJBgkqhkiG9w0BBwEwH-gYJYIZIAWUDBAEuMBEEDGtq24gy4zrcskpWJgIBEICBm_Qvs-GoXByDDrs0NzMsZ5G2pqo5Tsyu3wl0x8VSqGu_ifWGf_dJSt-gGhzxZVTjeH2NLFVlbDiXKdFVKiObLkkybyohMAtSymrbE1p-aOU_sqEvpmF9RG-qD-1Z2ITPFnDkMxMkL9ZMRt_qVLSN_ u61aGt7TqTX5-3C71AsnmMVEgFyhbAyo80UcwqGxkKqTtzEnF-GWVhRa6cv3OFy https://www.forbes.com/sites/hbsworkingknowledge/2012/12/30/competition-leads-to-workplace-corruption-research-shows/?sh=42aa230e4965

Stephenson, Matthew. (2014, July 3rd). GAB, The Global Anticorruption Blog. "Corruption and Liberalization: Two Paradoxes." https://globalanticorruptionblog.com/2014/07/03/corruption-and-liberalization-two-paradoxes/

Sumah, Stephan. (2018, February 21st). Corruption, Causes and Consequences. IntechOpen. https://www.intechopen.com/chapters/58969

Taylor, Alison. (2015). Best of 2015: Organizational Culture in Corrupt Companies. Corporate Compliance Insights. https://www.corporatecomplianceinsights.com/best-of-2015-organizational-culture-in-corrupt-companies/

Trade Commissioner Service. (2016, July). "Paying the price: Confronting Corruption in international business". Government of Canada. https://www.tradecommissioner.gc.ca/canadexport/0000655.aspx-?lang=eng

Transparency International. (February 4, 2022). 2021 Corruption Perception Index- Explore the results. https://www.transparency.org/en/cpi/2021

Tutorialspoint. Simply Easy Learning. (2022). "Liberalization vs Deregulation." https://www.tutorialspoint.com/international_business_management/liberalization.htm#

The dark mechanics of private sector corruption: Understanding the impact of supply-side corruption and how to tackle it. (2021). Strategic Direction, Bradford 37(11), 13-15. Emerald Publishing Limited. https://doi.org/10.1108/SD-10-2021-0116

Conclusion

It is clear that corruption is a pervasive and complex problem that affects every aspect of our lives. It undermines trust in institutions, erodes the rule of law, and hinders economic development. It is also a problem that is difficult to eradicate, as it is often fueled by greed, power, and a lack of transparency. As we move forward, it is important that we continue to educate ourselves about the many forms of corruption that exist and the ways in which we can work to combat them. Only through a better understanding of this complex issue can we hope to create a more just and equitable world for all.

www.ingramcontent.com/pod-product-compliance
Lightning Source LLC
Chambersburg PA
CBHW030118170426
43198CB00009B/656